$100,000 and Above

The New Realities of Executive Job Hunting

By Bob Gerberg
Princeton/Masters Press

About the Author

Bob Gerberg has a BA degree from Colgate University and an MBA degree from the University of Pittsburgh. After several years as an Air Force officer, he had a successful career with major food companies, including positions as a Vice President of Marketing Services and Assistant to the Chairman of a Fortune 500 company. Active in the career field for more than a decade, he has authored dozens of publications and cassettes on career transition.

Princeton/Masters is a high-level outplacement consulting firm with offices and associates in major cities. The firm's specialty is in designing and managing private marketing campaigns for six-figure executives.

Library of Congress Catalog Card Number 96-092339
ISBN 1-882885-07-4 (cloth)

Books by Princeton/Masters Press are available at quantity discounts. For information, write: Princeton/Masters Press Inc., 7951 E. Maplewood, Suite 333, Englewood, CO 80111; or call 800-772-4446.

Table of Contents

At Princeton / Masters International we create and manage private marketing campaigns for executives. Our work is a more sophisticated form of what some people call executive outplacement.

Once our firm is retained, the material in this book is usually communicated prior to commencing the customized part of our work for each individual. Properly applied, the principles can bring results that are dramatically superior to what traditional job hunting approaches yield.

I wish to thank the dozens of recruiters, HR Directors, clients and staff who have shared their observations. With best wishes for your success.   — Bob Gerberg

1

Today's Executive Job Market and Where the Jobs Are

The new reality: The numbers have changed dramatically. Yes, more executive jobs... but the number of competitors has accelerated at a faster pace. If you haven't looked for a job in a while, it's a whole new ball game.

With a U.S. population of more than 260,000,000 people, and a total job market approaching 130,000,000, opportunities at more than $100,000 can be clearly defined. Here are the numbers of jobs in the U.S. that currently reward people with earnings at this level (the figures are exclusive of revenues from interest, dividends, and capital gains):

2,512,000 jobs at $100K – $199K . . . (1.90%)
636,000 jobs at $200K – $499K . . . (0.50%)
122,000 jobs at $500K – $999K . . . (0.10%)
58,000 jobs at $1,000K + ... (0.04%)

A significant percentage of the people earning this level of income are doctors, lawyers, consultants, entertainment industry types (including authors and those associated with professional athletics), and entrepreneurs who run their own companies. However, there exists an equal number of people who have real earnings at this level but fail to report much of their income, as they take advantage of substantial perks and expenses rather than receiving pure wages.

"The number of executive jobs and the amounts of executive pay are both expanding at a very nice rate. The problem is that the number of job seekers is growing a lot faster."

— Larry Mingle, Executive Recruiter,
Formerly with Norman Broadbent and Russell Reynolds

The executive job market is strong, and the jobs are with smaller businesses

The executive job market has changed dramatically in recent years. Over the last five years, while much of the media attention was given to corporate downsizing, the six-figure job market grew more than 27%. Of these three million plus jobs, where people earn $100,000 or more, the best estimate is that 27,000 (0.8%) are now coming available each month. The market is supported by turnover, new businesses and new industries, and the small number of positions that become available as newly created positions.

During the last decade most opportunities have been with smaller businesses rather than with blue chip companies. Obviously, there will continue to be many fine opportunities that become available with the nation's leading organizations; however, in many cases they will occur only from retirements, terminations, and turnover.

The following statistics will give you some idea of the number of employers out there for you — aside from the national headquarters of larger organizations. Let's look at two major metropolitan areas. In San Francisco/Oakland, with a population of about four million, 171,000 employers have up to 99 employees, and 2,200 have more than 100.

In Houston, with a population of about 3.6 million, 131,000 employers have up to 99 employees, while 2,100 have more than 100. The employers with between five and 100 employees include companies in many of America's newest and fastest growing industries. If your career has been rooted in large companies, then some new thinking might be in order.

"In 1996, 3,000,000 new U.S. jobs will be created. Firms with under 5,000 employees will account for 94% and those with less than 100 employees will account for 66%. Small business is where the growth is." — Dun & Bradstreet Survey

The competition

While the number of executive jobs is growing, the competition is growing at a faster rate. Every year our population expands, and every year people are living longer and looking to work longer. The net result is that, at any one moment in time, the number of executives (and about-to-be executives) who are circulating resumes has grown to exceed *dozens of times* the available positions. This also reflects continuing uncertainty about job security.

So while the jobs are there, the bottom line is that today's executive job market is intensely competitive. Many people stand to lose $2,000, $3,000, $4,000 or more every week that they may be out of work. So if you are seeking a new career at this level, understanding what you are up against, and what you need to do to gain a competitive advantage can be very critical indeed.

Over the last decade, more than a third of all U.S. companies were restructured, several hundred thousand firms were downsized, and over 100,000 were acquired. What's more, half a million businesses failed, in addition to almost a million that sought bankruptcy protection.

It is with this in mind that the Princeton/Masters philosophy requires that people draw some completely new boundaries concerning their marketing approach. If you do this, your outlook can be very positive. This is especially true because one of the lessons about careers that we have learned is that each person has a reservoir of knowledge and skills that are either unknown or untapped... and which simply need to be identified and properly marketed.

"If you are an expert on derivatives, the Internet or a software engineer, you're in short supply. If you're anyone else, you've got a lot of competition."

— William Oldham, VP, Investment Banking Company

2

Traditional Job Hunting
Doesn't Work Anymore

The new reality: Most executives still just throw together a resume, answer some ads, and just visit a few recruiters and friends. However, their out-of-date approaches don't work well in the new executive job market. This opens the door for you to have a major competitive advantage.

M ost executives start by preparing a "tombstone resume" that typically says, "Here lies John Doe, went to these schools, had these jobs." Then, once they get their resumes together, they just scatter them as they answer some ads or visit a few recruiters or personal contacts. Some send out mass mailings using poor materials, the wrong lists, and the wrong techniques. In short, their approach is haphazard, expensive, full of dead-end leads, and they end up job hunting for a long, long time.

The statistics below summarize the recent average experience of men and women in search of executive positions. These were people who had been forced out of work via downsizing. Here is the average number of months from the date of their notification until they started in a new job:

Scientific	20.7
General management	17.7
Legal / consulting	16.6
Human resources	15.9
Accounting / finance	15.1
Misc. staff positions	14.9
Operations	14.7
Office management	13.8
Marketing / sales	13.8
Engineering & related	12.3
Information systems	12.1

In a recent article, *Business Week* also said executives who lost jobs should plan on 18 months of unemployment, and the U.S. Labor Department has been quoted as saying it takes a year or more. One of the reasons, however, is that as important as contacts and networking can be, most people rely far too much on these methods for uncovering new situations. This is clearly underscored by the data below.

When they land a position, the way in which their "traditional methods" enable them to find their positions may surprise you:

60% from existing contacts and direct referrals
22% from networking efforts (indirect referrals)
9% through contact with executive recruiters
5% from contacting employers directly
1% through answering advertisements
3% by all other means

So, in today's environment of faded loyalty and greater competition, just how should you approach your next career move? The reality is that executive job hunting can be handled on a faster, more convenient, and more predictable basis. However, there are some requirements.

The Princeton/Masters approach to executive job hunting

Your starting point is to recognize that the revolution in personal computers, databases, the Internet, and other sources of information can have a dramatic and positive impact on your potential for job-hunting success. So it's essential to capitalize on the remarkable communication and information tools that are available. They truly make it possible for people to take control of their own destiny

---

"I think the hidden reality is that it takes six-figure executives 1.5 months for every $10,000 they are seeking, but no one is going to admit it." — Lance Wright, HR, Mobil Oil

instead of playing the waiting game. We believe in a system that emphasizes new and well-organized approaches for going to your markets. We call it "proactive" rather than passive job hunting. To begin with you need to be willing to put aside your old ideas on job hunting. You need to bring a positive attitude to the table, a will to succeed, and a commitment to taking the necessary action to ensure your success. Here are the steps that are part of our professional job-hunting system.

Marketable assets. The first step involves uncovering all your marketable assets. There is more to this statement than meets the eye, and we will address ways for expanding your marketability beyond your obvious credentials. You will also be introduced to our concept of a personal communications strategy—a key element in political campaigns and equally important to making every career search a success.

Career and industry options. The second step involves knowing your options. Many people have found that crucial career or industry changes have brought them more challenge and satisfaction. Chances are, new career and industry options can be uncovered for you, as well as advanced opportunities within your career path.

Superior resumes and letters. The third step that's required is that you must have superior creative materials. This is extremely critical. A series of superior biographies, in combination with some well-designed marketing letters, can easily bring you 700% to 1,000% more activity than one standard resume and cover letter you might have used. In short, the right written materials can dramatically impact your career search possibilities.

"It's difficult to find the right talent from a technical side. From the managerial side, there's an unbelievable surplus."
— Carl Bruce, CEO, Unisource Corporation

An action plan for getting interviews. If you have a plan, you'll know which types of actions to take, and where, when, and how. This material will review the major channels you should consider and the basics of what you should do.

A game plan for interviewing. Let's face it, for every situation, there are likely to be a number of others under consideration. So obviously you must come across better than others. With our system, you'll find a series of steps which will allow you to maximize your chemistry in every interview and to handle objections in the smoothest possible way.

A negotiation process. We will introduce you to an easy-to-use process for negotiating. It has been all that many others have needed. I hope it will do the same thing for you.

In summary, methods from the 80s don't work very well anymore. But, then again, old marketing approaches don't work in any field. In recent articles, *Harvard Business Review*'s "Marketing is Everything" and *Business Week*'s "Value Marketing" both emphasized that smart marketing requires doing different things. Sony's founder, Masaru Ibuka, said, "The key to success for Sony, and to everything else in business, is never to follow the others." This is also sound advice for every job seeker.

"Most executives are totally unprepared to market themselves. Many do virtually nothing. They rely on a few select contacts to help and lose thousands of dollars in the process."

— Bill Kaiser, Divisional VP HR, Detergent Manufacturer

3

How to Expand Your Marketability Beyond Your Credentials

The new reality: To be competitive, you'll need more than a good background. The key is to capture everything about yourself that's marketable, and then build an appeal beyond your obvious credentials. Here's our philosophy on how to do it.

Are you thinking that your credentials are so strong, your resume so good, that a job will be yours for the asking? Maybe it should be that way, but surprisingly, the "best-qualified" people don't always make the winner's circle. Who does? Those who do the best job of marketing their strengths, their skills—themselves.

If you are like most executives, you can increase your chances through a very simple point of view. It has been said time and again by psychologists, motivational speakers, spiritual leaders and coaches, that the most restrictive limits you face are those you put on yourself. So, if you really want to be a serious candidate for a better position or a new career, don't put any limits on your thinking.

We have learned that everyone's experience is more marketable than they realize. In this discussion, we will review a number of ways to a broader view of your total experience and how you can describe it to potential employers.

Your marketable knowledge is broader than you think

First, assume that all aspects of your knowledge are marketable. For example, do you have knowledge of a job, a product, a process, or a market? It could come from work, hobbies, alumni relationships, reading or activities, or from suppliers, customers, friends, or your social life.

Your personality, character, interests, and enthusiasm are marketable

Personality, of course, is just a word for that mysterious combination of traits that can either attract us to someone quite strongly, or on the other hand, leave us unimpressed.

More employment decisions are based on personality and chemistry than any other factor. When this happens, the employer is probably thinking: *"He's certainly professional and quick-thinking. I like him, and better yet, I trust him. He'll get along with our team and provide leadership. I need to get him in this firm."*

Your interests and enthusiasm are also marketable. How many employers do you suppose hire people primarily because they showed great interest in their business? *The answer is, a lot!*

The opportunity you represent is also marketable

If you can make an employer aware of an opportunity that you can exploit, or a problem that you can help solve, you can create a job for yourself. Of course, if the employer is aware of the need or opportunity, all you need to do is let them know that you're the right person to handle it.

Some executives view their previous jobs as having a narrow focus, and you may be thinking, *"I don't have a lot of options."* However, you can expand your appeal and uncover more options. The idea is to uncover "any experience you've had" in a way that makes the experience more transferable.

"Versatility is the name of the game. Executive jobs are being redefined — it's all about moving from one project to another and handling a lot of balls at one time."

— Ron Kessler, Management Supervisor, Advertising Agency

Besides your functional experience, your transferable skills are marketable

Identifying transferable skills is critical. For example, analyzing, organizing, group presentation skills, problem solving, and so on. In the current job market, employers are clearly placing a premium on men and women who are versatile. The parameters around many jobs have changed as layers of management have been eliminated. Those who are perceived as being of great potential value are those who can move from project to project, handling assignments that draw upon different skills.

Because it is unrealistic for people to think in terms of job security, the best way to currently protect yourself and your career is to be seen as a versatile team player capable of being a "money maker" in many different situations. In fact, it is a rare individual who can move ahead and stay ahead with a single predominant skill.

Naturally, your experience can also be reviewed according to various "functions" that apply to most businesses, such as sales, production, accounting, marketing, human resources. At the same time, you need to think of your experience in terms of "action verbs" that describe what you did and that translate those activities into achievements. For example, *controlled, scheduled, wrote, improved, reshaped, built, created,* etc.

The more ways you describe your experience, the more you will qualify for jobs in many career fields and industries. That's because all organizations are basically involved in similar functions. So, look at your experience from a few different slants.

Having a communications strategy is very critical

With the approach just described, you'll set the stage to build appeal beyond your factual credentials. However, you'll also need to follow a communications plan controlling how you want to be perceived. Your need for this can best be appreciated by comparing it to the "platform" of a candidate for the Presidency. The "platform" anticipates questions on major issues by formulating carefully-thought-out position statements to guide the candidate's answers.

Our philosophy involves identifying the "core" words and phrases that will be the heart of your communications strategy. These words should become a regular part of "your story" that you communicate to employers, recruiters, and others who might be of help. Please realize that your "tickets" alone (advanced degrees, blue-chip background, titles, etc.) will not necessarily motivate another employer to hire you. Those credentials offer only one form of reassurance that suggests you are right for the job. This is why you must use words that add interest beyond your credentials.

Now, when any of us recruit people, we usually have a concept in mind. In the final analysis, we hire others for the traits, skills, and abilities that certain key descriptive phrases imply. So, it's important to select those that set you apart. For example, you may have *operated effectively under pressure.* Perhaps you are *an excellent motivator* or you may have *built highly effective teams.*

Most executives can identify at least 30 key words and concepts. Used appropriately, these words and concepts can set you apart from the competition and convey the unique advantages you have to offer. To help illustrate, here are some key phrases: *entrepreneurial strengths; experience in a growth company; resourceful problem-solver; intuitive decision-maker; experienced in formulating policy; ability to inspire others to peak performance; built profits in international operations*; and so on.

Make sure your leadership
appeal is evident to others

Much has been written about America's search for leadership at all levels of business. And if there is one quality you want to be able to communicate, leadership ability is it. But just how is leadership projected, especially if you're not a celebrity in the business world?

An article that appeared in United Airlines' in-flight magazine examined the qualities necessary to be perceived as a leader in today's environment. The observations included much of the following: Most experts say that real leaders possess and communicate real convictions. These are seen as strong feelings and principles that have grown with them over time. Obviously, those convictions need to match the requirements of the organization and those who might follow.

Whether it's justified or not, leadership is also attributed to those who create an image of operating at the far edge of the frontier — where new products and solutions are being planned for the future. We tend to think of leaders as those who have vision and the ability to develop new things or bring the best improvements to older ones.

Other attributes that people ascribe to leaders are that they are creative, intuitive, and passionate, and that they project integrity, trust, and boldness. Image, attitude, appearance, and presence can all play a role. Put all of these traits together, and they represent most of the criteria that contribute to people being viewed as charismatic.

"To expand marketability you just need to give some examples of leadership. That's been a missing ingredient in our organization, and it's the one most desperately needed in other companies." — VP HR, Automotive Company

The right stories will be essential
to expanding your appeal

Another key to expanding your marketability has to do with your ability to develop stories to make yourself sound more interesting. Most people who interview you will forget what you say in a matter of minutes. To ensure that your points are both memorable and credible, use a technique for creating interesting "stories."

SODAR is an acronym that stands for Situation, Opportunities, Duties, Actions, and Results. It represents a process of describing your past experience in a way that resembles a motion picture. Here's how you can use it:

❑ <u>Situation</u>. Describe a job by reviewing the situation when you began, making it sound interesting.

❑ <u>Opportunities</u>. Then bring up information about the opportunities that the job presented.

❑ <u>Duties</u>. Subsequently, you describe your duties.

❑ <u>Actions</u>. More importantly, you should quickly move to actions taken by you and others (the team).

❑ <u>Results</u>. Then relate what results occurred.

SODAR means "telling the whole story." If it's well told, it will generate more genuine interest than any recitation of duties. Of course, the R in SODAR (results) is the most important. Try to quantify the results. For example, you cut costs by $100,000 or 20%. Remember, don't be modest.

Try to describe results in terms of dollars or percent increases. Indicate any good things you did to help your organizations and how you took on extra tasks. Describe how you helped your superiors meet their goals, and also the results they achieved. Develop stories that cover situations where you can demonstrate the value of fresh thinking as a means to improving productivity, or show that you have solved a wide variety of problems in diverse areas.

Age doesn't need to be
the barrier you think it is

The biggest concern about marketability for many people has to do with their age. Obviously, age will affect job seekers, but this too can be handled. As American business has been getting leaner over the last decade, there has been a noticeable trend toward the hiring of younger executives.

As businesses and companies have been re-engineered, many people in their 50s and early 60s have seen their jobs eliminated or replaced. A look at the Annual Report issued by PepsiCo, Inc., one of America's top 20 corporations in market value, gives perhaps a good example of the trend:

CEO of Pepsi Cola, North America . . . . . age 49
CEO of Frito Lay, Inc. . . . . age 46
CEO of PepsiCo Foods/Beverages, Int . . . age 44
CEO of Pizza Hut, Inc. . . . . age 51
CEO of Taco Bell Corp. . . . . age 49
CEO of Kentucky Fried Chicken . . . . . . age 42
CEO of PepsiCo Restaurants, Int. . . . . . age 42
CEO of PepsiCo Food Systems . . . . age 46
CEO of PepsiCo Worldwide Rest's . . . . . . age 50

The same report listed 36 corporate officers of PepsiCo, Inc. The median age was 47. Of those, 8 were in their 30s, 14 were in their 40s, 12 were in their 50s, and 2 were 60 or more. The new CEO of PepsiCo, Roger Enrico, is 51.

If you are in a situation where you think your age may be a problem, then a more aggressive action plan for getting interviews will be required.

"The use of carefully rehearsed stories impresses people. Anyone who has listened to a speech or a sales presentation knows how interesting it is if the speaker uses short stories to demonstrate a point."

— Michele Lutz, President, Princeton/Masters Client Services

Now from a professional viewpoint, there are different things that we undertake to help our clients get the most out of their marketability. However, they all have to do with the principles of dealing with the factors brought up in this discussion. We start by asking our clients to complete a *Career History and Marketability Profile* (CHAMP). A remarkable device, it gives us insight into people by having them check words and phrases that might describe them, their achievements, their skills, and their approaches to various situations. Through it, people take a fresh new view of their career experiences. Independently, your approach should be the same.

Remember, these are the primary ways for expanding your marketability. First, you can broaden your appeal by communicating your experience according to (a) business functions, (b) your skills and duties, and (c) your achievements. In addition, because your knowledge and interests are marketable, it's essential to surface any special interests that might appeal to employers. Naturally, your personality, character, and enthusiasm can also be marketable (something many people overlook), as well as the opportunity you represent and the types of problems you can help an employer solve.

A major key to building appeal beyond your credentials is the use of a "communications plan." Here, you identify words that reflect your special strengths. Then, you develop the key phrases that describe your traits, skills, abilities, and qualities that employers look for. You follow through by using them in all written and verbal communications. To make your experiences more interesting and memorable, use them with the storytelling concept I've described.

"If you're in your 50s or older, you need to run a campaign that is broader and that focuses you on more career and industry options. Then you'll need to be more aggressive."
— Tom Smith, President, Princeton/Masters Northern CA

4

Uncovering Your Most Exciting Industry Options

The new reality: More executives than ever change industries, and many go on to greater success. Don't shortchange yourself by taking a narrow view of your options. It's a pretty exciting world out there.

When you are thinking about changing jobs, you need to take a close look at yourself, your career field, and the industry you're working in. For better or worse, in our world of work you will quickly find that when compared to a decade ago, you have changed, your career field has changed, and your industry has changed.

In today's job market most people must be prepared to market themselves with sufficient skill so that they may be viewed as attractive to employers in a variety of industries.

Why not consider growth industries?

What are some of the fast-growing industries? Well, they include such industries as personal computers, software, microchips, entertainment, telecommunications, certain media, biotechnology, physical therapy/fitness, special education, security/private investigation, sports, and anything to do with the Internet, to name a few.

In 1982, the personal computer industry was a $1 billion industry. Today, it is estimated to be more than a $150 billion industry. During this period, the industry has had many ups and downs, but total employment has dramatically expanded.

While many firms have been through profit squeezes and layoffs, an individual who joined an industry during the last decade would now have a substantial range of employer possibilities competing for his or her talents.

Another reason for seeking out growth industries involves their need to go outside their industry to meet their employment needs. For example, in the early 80s the cable television industry was in a phase of explosive growth. The CEOs of these firms could not find enough executives with cable television experience to meet their companies' growth objectives. As a result, opportunities abounded for high-level professionals from varied backgrounds. These firms simply hired the best natural talent.

80% of executives who change jobs consider new industry options

Despite the recession of the early 90s, new companies are springing up throughout America. Established organizations are reexamining the way they do business. Medium-sized companies are expanding. New industries now exist that are employing tens of thousands.

Needless to say, the more you appear to know about an industry, the easier it is to generate interviews. For example, do you have experience in or knowledge of similar product lines, distribution channels, manufacturing methods, or problems within an industry?

There can be other similarities. Consider the scope of operations, the role of advertising and promotion, the importance of the field-sales organization, or the influence of

---

"The three hardest industry changes: moving out of government, out of education, or out of the armed services. Other industry changes are no longer unusual, or that difficult."
— Patricia Maynard, HR Consultant, Marriott Hotels

labor. The harder it is to demonstrate knowledge of an industry, the less likely a person is to move into it. Here are some industry changes that are commonplace:

■ *A client of ours was a marketing executive with a tobacco company, and she joined a cosmetics firm. Why? Their methods of marketing are similar.*

■ *Another client was the EVP of a circuit-board company, and was recruited to become president of a firm that makes power packs. Why? These industries have similarities in manufacturing and sales.*

■ *An aerospace executive was recruited to become CEO of a small firm that sells high-tech services to defense contractors. Why? The key was the new CEO's contacts and his knowledge of the market.*

If you have no knowledge of an industry but would like to explore situations, extra steps are recommended. The easiest way to acquire knowledge of a new industry is to read trade publications. It's surprisingly easy to be able to communicate on personnel changes, new products, information on specific companies, and the major challenges as seen by industry leaders.

Another way is to talk with people already in the field. In some cases, you can go further by getting more formal input, attending trade shows, and the like. The most radical approach is to accept a lower-level job in an industry in order to acquire knowledge.

Now, troubled industries can also have something to offer. During the last decade we've witnessed declines in a succession of industries. However, you should never overlook opportunities in troubled industries. Executives who have worked for firms under pressure often find that they can be valuable to distributors or to consulting firms. Those who learned tough lessons in competitive battles can function as veterans in any industry.

Confidence is critical —
don't underrate yourself

Transition to a new industry is much easier than it used to be. Historically, people tend to overrate the barriers and to underrate their own abilities to make contributions in new areas in a relatively short time frame. As you review potential industries, you might also remember that while glamorous high-tech and service businesses receive 90% of the publicity today, many people will find far more opportunities in industries that are considered low-tech or non-glamorous by today's standards.

Obviously, you need to be sure not to overlook your leverage power. Here I am referring to the added benefits you may bring by virtue of your contacts or knowledge. You may be able to bring a complete team with you that helped you "turn around" a similar situation. Perhaps you control major accounts who would give you their business in a new field. Or it's possible you have cut millions from overhead before and know exactly how you would do it again.

Your versatility can also be a major consideration. The fact is, nearly every capable person can work in a different function that is broader, narrower, or in some way associated with a past position. Here are some examples that will reinforce this point:

■ *A versatile purchasing executive found it easy to move to a position where she is responsible for all manufacturing; and a general manager became the marketing VP for a consumer goods firm in another industry.*

■ *An executive switched to big-ticket computer sales because of his experience; and a lending officer became the top executive in a financial services firm.*

"There isn't a growth industry in America that doesn't hire people from other industries. There's no other solution to our requirements." — Robert Nelson, Sr. VP HR, Software Firm

Be sure to communicate the scope of your knowledge and potential. Sales executives, for instance, usually know quite a bit about marketing, human resources, and distribution. Manufacturing professionals often know a great deal about administration, the control function, and general management. A controller may often have a grasp of every aspect of his/her business.

When you are discussing the requirements for a position, it will be important for you to distinguish between arbitrary requirements and those that really relate directly to results. Arbitrary requirements include degrees, length of time in positions, previous titles, and specific industry experience. However, the final hiring decision usually has little to do with specifications. If you can present yourself convincingly as being able to produce results, you will likely get the job. Here are some more examples:

■ *An executive went from government to president of a pharmaceutical company; and a lawyer from the steel business became EVP of an engineering company. The CEO of a public corporation became president of a Wall Street firm; and the EVP of a utility became COO of a diversified manufacturer.*

There are thousands of examples, and at all income levels. If you believe you can produce direct results in a given situation, be sure you lay claim to it. Too many people seek out positions at a lower level than they should, or they rule themselves out of a job they could do well simply because they have never done it before.

If you are switching industries, you will find that, generally speaking, more opportunities emerge in the small and mid-sized companies. They don't have layers of management waiting to fill new opportunities. Also, their executives tend to be less specialized, making it possible for you to fill a more versatile role.

To recap, many people are afraid to move out of their industry specialty. However, every month thousands of executives start careers in new industries — areas where they had no direct previous experience. Once you've had experience in two or three industries, your marketability is also greater than ever before. And, chances are, your capability for changing industries may now be more important than ever before.

For each of our clients, we have a process of analysis for coming up with all of the areas they should explore. It starts with a review of thousands of industries. Then, we use many sophisticated databases to screen the hundreds of smaller or faster-growing industries that might be of interest in each individual case. The end result is that having analyzed someone's background and by applying the type of thinking described in this chapter, we are able to come up with a range of industries for which they might be good candidates.

Most people are quite unaware of the enormous range of industries that are growing rapidly. When you screen industries as possibilities for yourself, the process is just as I've outlined in this discussion. Essentially, you are looking for some similarities to the areas in which you've had experience. These can take the form of similarities in distribution channels, marketing and sales approaches, manufacturing, whether they are capital intensive or people intensive, and so on. This common sense approach may be all you need to significantly broaden your horizons.

"You need to identify all the ways you can be of value. The key today is being multifaceted. Stop thinking only of those things for which you had direct responsibility."
— Narisimha Dela, Former VP, Chase Manhattan Int'l

5

The Seven Most Popular Executive Career Changes

The new reality: Most people have changed careers more than once. In the future, having several good careers will become standard fare. You should be aware of the most popular choices.

As mentioned in the last chapter, people not only undergo change themselves, but their career fields can change dramatically. Areas that once offered great opportunity can be financially confining. Does advertising offer the same possibilities as it did a decade ago? Does selling in the steel industry? Does being a doctor in sports medicine? The obvious answer is no.

Many people view themselves solely by what they've done in the past. However, every month thousands of executives start new careers — areas in which they have no previous experience. However, if you take a narrow view of yourself, you could be making a mistake. If you see yourself as a specialist, you may believe you are locked into a given career. Or you may feel you have few options because you are too much of a generalist.

Believe it or not, there are 22,000 different job titles in use today, but 95% of all professionals fall within a few hundred career specialties. Nevertheless, when most people make a major change, they frequently explore one of the following popular options:

Owning a franchise

This has become the standard alternative for hundreds of thousands of executives. The number of franchises available has multiplied dramatically as more than 4,000 companies in 120 industries offer franchises today.

Consulting

The knowledge business as a whole has been booming. Success in this field rests squarely on your ability to attract and maintain clients. If selling is not your suit, but you are convinced you have a great deal to offer, you will have to attract one or more partners or employees who will devote their time to the sales side of your enterprise.

Some of the most popular consulting specialties include finance, marketing, new product development, data processing and systems, executive search and outplacement, cost reduction, and public relations. There is also good activity in labor relations, electrical engineering, design, and other technical disciplines. If you would rather join an existing firm, it is an easier way to get started than striking out on your own, and you can benefit from the experience. Regardless of the type of consulting you choose, remember that the special knowledge that makes a consultant valuable today may be obsolete several years later. So you need to keep current in your field. If you enjoy variety and intellectual challenge, then consulting can be your right move.

Being a producer

The third most popular career change is when people become producers. These are sales jobs where you bring in business. Some examples include executive recruiters, financial planners, stockbrokers, real estate brokers, outplacement specialists, etc. If you have contacts and need a shift, this kind of role can be attractive. There are opportunities for producers in every discipline. Approximately 10 percent of our labor force is involved in sales.

" I've known five people who have changed careers recently. Three went into consulting; two started their own businesses. Most executive career changes fit a similar pattern."
— Greg Larson, Senior HR Manager, Marathon Oil

Starting a new venture

Many people have ideas and knowledge or access to a facility that can provide the basis for a new venture. Perhaps you have an idea about a product around which you can develop a marketing or business plan. Can you put together financing beyond your own investment? Do you want to own? Or, do you want to invest and sell?

Partnership options are popular. Experience dictates that they work best when you choose someone whose skills complement your own or who has investment money to make a business grow. Purchasing smaller companies on an outright basis can also offer unique advantages to those with an entrepreneurial instinct. You can put a personal stamp on such enterprises or stay in a passive role.

Despite many "killer category" national chains, certain specialty stores can still be candidates for purchase. Popular choices include garden shops, nurseries, specialty sporting goods stores and marinas, and products involving computers or software, men's clothing, or even gourmet foods and wines. The possibilities could include small restaurants and inns, theaters, printing and travel services, manufacturing plants, apartments, hotels, and numerous family businesses. Real estate investing has become an increasingly sophisticated field. The packages may involve vacant land, commercial buildings, single- or multiple-family residences, abandoned factories, government repossessions, etc.

"General management consulting, EDP consulting, executive search and outplacement are good for generalists. You need to be able to attract new business. Phone contact and travel are drawbacks, but the pay can be good."

— Bart Kellerher, HR Manager, Bell Atlantic

Directorships

Many people who can bring prestige and experience to smaller corporations become sought after for directorships. A seventh major area for career change... for a small percentage it can represent a full time occupation. However, it usually takes some planning to get started. When you have served on one board, it is far easier to engineer an invitation to join others.

In fact, directorships with just several corporations, along with committee work, can often provide adequate income and lots of challenge. Some stock exchanges can direct you to clearinghouse services for executives interested in directorships. It is also possible to run a campaign aimed at existing directors, investment bankers, lawyers, and CEOs by discreetly inquiring whether your services might be valuable to one or more of the companies with which they are associated. Obviously, this avenue is most feasible for those with strong reputations. However, even if this is not the case, it is possible to develop opportunities. Think carefully of what you have to offer that would set you apart.

If you are known as someone who can increase productivity or cut costs, or if you have proven talents in securing financing, making acquisitions, or entering new markets, then it will be easy for many board members and CEOs to envision you making contributions.

The secretary to the CEO, current Directors, and even the corporate secretary may be aware of these openings, and be a good person to contact. Turnover tends to be at its peak in late winter and early spring, and a lengthy biography is a must. In cases like this, it is wise to decide on some limits as to how many companies you can help in this capacity. Because directorships now carry more exposure to liability, corporations no longer expect directors to serve for just a nominal sum or without proper insurance.

Writing or lecturing

Another popular area for career change includes commercial writing or lecturing. Each year over 40,000 new books are published. A more important option for writers involves preparing articles that might be accepted by some of the country's 11,000+ trade and business magazines. The lecture circuit can also be appealing to specialists. Agents can, for a percentage, arrange engagements. Top rates are reserved for those with celebrity status. However, thousands make an interesting career out of the lecture circuit.

Non-profits and education

A very popular alternative for many business people who change careers involves working in nonprofits or the education field. More than 20,000 trade organizations are run like businesses and have similar needs. On the administrative side, many executives have made contributions in helping to keep educational institutions solvent. In many respects, education is like any other service business. People must be recruited and trained, and facilities must be operated efficiently. Information systems and data processing are needed; funds must be raised and public image promoted.

Those with corporate experience will find they are of particular value in the graduate schools of business. In fact, a number of universities have former corporate officers as professors, administrators, heads of development and fundraising, and deans of their business schools. Here, an advanced degree is usually a prerequisite. Those who favor classroom teaching or lecturing may still find that they eventually gravitate to management.

"An increasing number of opportunities are available in our controversial, but challenging field of education. Relatively few business executives are aware of this."

— Mike McCall, Consultant, Former Professor of Business

In summary, as you consider new career options, weigh your answers to the following questions carefully. Have you identified an area that you really like? Can you differentiate yourself from competition? Do you have a special niche? Are you a hands-on type of person? Are you someone who can make decisions and move fast? Are you a good producer, recruiter, or motivator? Last, but not least, are you genuinely a resourceful type of person? If a possible career change is an interest of yours, some critical thinking is in order.

To assist clients we often will make use of profile instruments to help guide our thinking in this area. Many of these have come a long way in recent years. Then, after having a team analyze everything about a client that we can get our hands on, we begin by matching their personal profile against the 300 most common careers I mentioned earlier. If we don't find something there, we go deeper into the thousands of specialty careers that are commonly listed in various directories. The whole idea is to zero in on careers which may offer you what you want, and which makes the best use of your skills and knowledge.

Changing careers is nothing new. As many historians have pointed out, Thomas Jefferson had more than eight different careers. Chances are, there are several new careers that might be worth your exploration.

6

The Only Style of Resume You Should Ever Use

The new reality: People who are out there with an assembly-line resume will wait a long time for lightning to strike. Several biographies and a variety of custom letters are what's required today. They need to tell just the right story and be all set for use with the different opportunities that are likely to present themselves.

I always used to marvel at how bad some people's resumes were, yet how well they did in the job market. Then one day I discovered that your need for a superior resume operated in reverse order to the following criteria.

First are those who have achieved celebrity status. Then there are those who are well-enough known, or who have relationships that help them land jobs immediately. Next are those who have an industry hook or high-demand specialty. Needless to say, if you're an expert on my business and I can use help, then let's talk. Last are the top producers in any field, the people who can simply call and say, "This is what I've done for others, I'm a pro, I can do the same or better for you."

Now, if you fit into one of the above categories, you are in good shape. If you are in the other 97% — then the information that follows is very important. The number of resumes circulated, relative to the number of attractive positions, is going up. As I've said, hundreds of people are apt to answer every good ad, and as many as 4,000 resumes arrive at executive search firms each month. In short, the competition is intense and will continue to increase.

When you look for a job, you are reduced to how you look on paper. Nevertheless, 95% of all resumes are far less effective than they could be. They are average in appearance, disclose too many liabilities, and are rarely interesting. Worst of all, a single resume is usually expected to work with all types of audiences, and it doesn't.

A narrative style
of resume is the best of all

After reviewing hundreds of thousands of resumes, we have a good handle on what works best for executives. The answer: narrative resumes that are written in a style that is similar to a letter.

The first reason a narrative is preferred is that it seems like less of a sales pitch than traditional resumes, which are full of dashes, bullets and too much bold type. I know how much our clients want good jobs, but one of the keys is to never appear too available. Who wants to hire someone who appears desperate or isn't wanted by others? The resumes that work best are ones that make you sound articulate, that never simply scream a bunch of facts, and that tell a persuasive story.

The second reason a narrative is best is that it appears more dignified and more professional. Needless to say, the closer it comes to a letter, the more personal and readable your resume will seem. At the same time, a narrative approach enables you to more easily avoid disclosing any liabilities you may have (things that might rule you out and you'll never know why).

The third reason in support of a narrative is that it is a "solution resume." Using this style, it is easier to craft a story in support of any objective you have. The same holds true for all the letters you might need in a job search. Once you have your narrative, adapting the same words and phrases to marketing letters is much easier as well.

A narrative resume will work best in the four situations that you are likely to encounter. One is when it is requested after you meet an employer — at the beginning of or during an interview. Another is when your resume is used as a leave-behind — after you've finished an interview, and when it is likely to be circulated to other people along with the impressions of the first party. A third is when it is provided for personal contacts to distribute. And a fourth is when it is sent out cold to employers or recruiters.

If you give a moment to thinking about these situations, looking at all the other styles you might use, you'll quickly see why a narrative is really the best solution — and truly the resume for all seasons.

The four popular ways
to arrange your presentation

The historical approach. This outlines your career in chronological order, starting with your most recent employer. It works best for those whose careers include a succession of increasingly responsible positions. Clearly it is preferred for the simple reason that it is far easier to read than information presented in other formats. If you want action from recruiters, an arrangement that reveals your factual history in a clear fashion is a must.

The achievement approach. This is most commonly used by people whose main accomplishments may not be in their most recent position. Here, your achievements are listed in the most persuasive language possible, with specific numbers, time-frames, and percentages used when describing them.

"I don't bother reading anything from executives that is not a historical resume. The vague approach favored by certain people doesn't do them any good with recruiters."
— Greg Peay, Executive Recruiter/President, Careers Ltd.

The functional approach. This communicates your career experience according to "business functions" (sales, accounting, etc.) It's great for generalists, career changers, people who were with one firm a long time, and those with too many jobs. This same functional style can be used to emphasize skills rather than functions; for example, your experience and achievements in directing turnarounds, boardroom presentations, complex analytical assignments, organizing new companies, etc.

The situation approach. This tells a story about four or five key situations. It gives fast-moving explanations of those situations and how you dealt with them. This format can be very effective for individuals who may be strong generalists as well as those in the highest echelons of corporate America.

Regardless of which of the arrangements you choose, an objective at the top of your resume, along with a short but compelling summary, is critical. This tells the reader that you are a person with a clear purpose, and it enables an employer to quickly assess you in terms of positions that may be available.

In your summary, you may choose to emphasize positive information on any aspect of your story, although most people will want to describe only work experience, education, and their most important personal assets. Having an objective and a summary will help ensure that your main selling points will almost always be read.

Too often people understate their contributions. So, take credit for larger achievements when you have played a key role in the overall effort. It's also important that you be presented as more interesting than your competition. You may also want to comment on issues that have emotional appeal; for example, commitment, values, motivation, professionalism, reputation, work style, and interpersonal skills, among others.

The number of biographies
that many executives require today

As the market has changed in the last decade, what people can expect from their written materials has changed as well. In today's competitive job market, you cannot run a sophisticated marketing campaign and expect one resume to be effective with each and every audience. To maximize interest in our clients, we typically create the following package of creative materials for each executive.

1 — A CEO / board member biography

This document tells each person's complete story, often being three, four, or even five pages, and is written in a third-person style. It can be very effective when circulated to high-level networking contacts, as well as CEOs, board members, heads of venture capital firms, and other senior executives.

More dignified than other resumes, this type of biography should also be supplied in situations once you are definitely under consideration. Since at that point your material will be carefully read, you want to put your best foot forward. Using a longer story at this point can also help speed things along, and sometimes negate the need for further checking on the employer's part.

2 — A mainstream biography

This is a highly distinctive narrative resume, usually two or three pages in length. It would be used in connection with direct mail, everyday networking, and in various situations where a resume is requested or advisable for introductory proposes.

"Contrary to what you might assume, when I was at Xerox, we really did review every executive resume."

— Doug Eiglehart, Management Consultant

3 — An executive recruiter resume

To be most effective with recruiter mailings, a factual and historical approach to highlighting your most marketable assets and skills is required. Once a recruiter shows interest, a CEO biography would be supplied.

4 — A spot opportunity resume

This unique document is graphically designed to allow room to conveniently pen a short note on the resume itself. People use this when they see a news event that suggests that their experience could be of help, when emerging situations are uncovered. Handwritten notes allow people to get more of these in circulation, and more quickly. The informal, but personal, handwritten style is very effective.

5 — Universal biographies

This is a term for resumes we supply to broaden a person's background, and qualify them for other opportunities. For example, a CFO may wish to explore senior operations positions, or a marketing VP might want to be considered for COO/general management positions. In these cases, separate resumes are often required to best qualify candidates for additional areas of interest.

The critical importance of written materials in an executive career search.

Marketing letters can often be just as important as resumes. For each of our clients, we typically draft about a dozen custom letters... with each one intended for use with a specific application. For example, we draft separate letters for answering ads, for sending in response to articles, for contacting influential people, for requesting a reference, for using in direct mail, for asking for referrals from acquaintances, for contacting recruiters, and so on.

Having everything prepared in advance is critical, so that our clients can focus on their campaign, rather than attempting to create materials when a situation arises. The goal is to help people respond to situations with more speed and convenience... and most importantly, with greater confidence and bottom-line results. On your own, you should approach your creative materials in the same manner — have them all drafted in advance.

Considering what's at stake with your career, your biographies need to be just right. Your communications must never undersell your capabilities or position you in an overly-narrow manner.

The kind of writing that is needed is not something that can be handled with an average effort. Remember, you are marketing a million-dollar product. What's required to do the job at your level starts with taking the time to analyze your career situation and all that you have to offer the marketplace. Obviously, you need to be clear on what your objectives are, and you need to have a way with words to create the documents you need.

There are two guiding concepts to this type of writing. First, it isn't just words that make the difference. The key is in the psychological impact beneath the words... the "subtleties" which help to motivate the right reaction at the receiving end. The second guiding concept concerns the fact that the unpublished job market is a "dormant" market... and remains so until triggered into responding. This happens when you use superior materials to contact the right person... in the right company... and at the right time. Now, unlike standard resumes, narratives can be tailored to cre-

---

"I'd say you can't go wild with resumes, or you will leave the impression that you're overselling. The best compromise is to be creative yet professional; low-key but look different."
— Gail Mendelson, Executive Recruiter

ate an image about you that says you are interesting, have certain skills and personal qualities... and that you simply are not like everyone else.

Your written materials also assist in other ways, even impacting the interviewing process. Let me share an analogy that illustrates this point. Let's assume a company invited a typical job seeker for an interview. Now, when that person walked in, chances are that they would only be 10% sold, and 90% of the hiring decision would rest on their ability to interview. This could put them under a lot of pressure.

To reduce pressure, your materials should be aimed at pre-selling you to the point of being 40–50% pre-sold into a position... rather than the customary 10%. The idea is to have employers sincerely want to see you. The reaction you want is, "John, I've been looking forward to seeing you. I have the feeling you can really be of help."

In closing, make sure your written materials are the very best they can be. They must be persuasive, visually distinctive and, of most importance, they must capture the best expression of your experience, skills, and potential.

"If you want to be successful, you need to beat your own drum. But you need to have just the right finesse. To be competitive today, your materials have to tell an extremely good story."
— John Sherrill, Former VP, Broadcasting Company

7

The Fastest Way for Finding Good Leads

The new reality: Private openings are signaled by events that are reported in the media. Your ability to recognize these leads and go after the opportunities they represent can make the difference.

*T*he following discussion is especially important for people who want to change careers or industries.

Why are over 90% of all executive jobs filled privately, and how do companies do this? Well, they seek to fill openings privately because it is an effective and less expensive method for finding quality people.

Most firms fill positions through personal referrals or by hiring someone who simply contacts them at the right time. By hiring in this manner, they avoid the costs of recruiter fees and advertising expenses.

Now, if you can learn where these openings exist, it stands to reason that you can have a major edge over your competitors. What's more, you might be able to have your credentials up for singular consideration, instead of applying right along with scores of others.

To find employers with unadvertised openings, all you need to do is follow events in the press. We call those situations "emerging opportunities." Of course, you can also uncover jobs that are not advertised through mailings, telemarketing, and networking, but following events in the press is the most direct way.

The right events are your key to uncovering emerging opportunities

Every day, in thousands of firms, events occur that ultimately lead employers to begin the process of privately looking for new people. These events are often reported in local and national business publications, trade magazines, newsletters, and newspapers. Here you will find articles on growth situations, new divisions, new facilities, new products, reorganizations, acquisitions, high-level executive changes, and plans for investments or expansion.

For companies undergoing these transitions, chances are they will need to attract good people to handle problems or capitalize on their opportunities. The activity in these companies won't usually be limited to one or two functions either.

While private openings are being filled by all types of employers, they are filled with far greater frequency in organizations experiencing significant change. Here's how a few executives have capitalized by uncovering openings through events:

■ *A financial executive learned that a troubled manufacturer was divesting a division. She called the new president and arranged to meet him. Four weeks later, she became the CFO of this company.*

■ *A marketing manager read that a European firm bought a local company. He wrote to express interest and suggested a dialogue when officials visited. Twelve weeks later, he was VP-Marketing, USA, at $120,000.*

When you read about a company that is giving off signals that it may be hiring at an above-average rate, don't stop at the obvious implications. Use "ripple-effect thinking." This is simply taking the time to think about all of the changes that may be occurring in the company — up and down the line and across many functions.

You may also get some good ideas about using information that you read about one company to find opportunities with a company's suppliers, customers, and even their competitors.

To take full advantage of emerging opportunities, consider the following example: You read that a manufacturer is starting a division to sell a new kind of packaging for protecting sensitive healthcare supplies. The obvious implications are that this company could very well need people in marketing and sales. Because it's a new division, you might also expect that there will be some need for accounting and finance people as well.

If you're a packaging engineer, you might also project a need for that capability to support the sales effort. Those possibilities would be real enough, but now use "ripple-effect thinking" to see if we can infer some other needs. For example, you may be someone who is experienced in dealing with regulatory authorities. You recognize that the potential sellers of this product will have to deal with them to gain product approval.

When you are seeking out new opportunities, you also don't want to overlook organizations with problems. Problems often imply one of two things: managers haven't been performing well, or the company needs to develop new capabilities in order to survive and grow.

Organizations with problems often need help from the following types of people: marketing people who can identify new markets and launch new products; financial executives who can cut costs or raise capital; general managers who can take responsibility; COOs who can supply new

---

"We're in telecommunications, and our industry is in real flux. We go outside for talent. Naturally, I prefer industry people, but it's all a matter of who comes to our attention."

— Marketing VP, Telecommunications Company

leadership; human resource executives who can help find all these other people.

Most of the time a CEO or a board member will be the logical person for you to contact. Keep in mind that many employers undergoing change are actually the smaller and faster-growing firms, and they are far less constrained by hiring traditions common to major companies. Organizations that are on a fast track will usually be looking for executives with the best natural ability and who have enthusiasm, dedication, and the right work ethic.

How to find events that are good leads to unadvertised jobs

For our clients, we access special databases that report on tens of thousands of business events that are written about in hundreds of media. We retrieve extracts by keywords... such as mergers, executive changes, sales growth, new products, and many other criteria. As reviewed in this chapter, these articles can often be your very best lead sources. Throughout your search, you need to stay abreast of emerging situations as identified in the business section of your local papers and in trade magazines. Remember, information is power, and that's exactly what news of emerging opportunities provides.

"Executive job hunting is all about one thing. Access to information is the name of the game."

— Roger Iverson, Former VP HR, Div. of American Cyanamid

8

How to Make the
Most of Executive Recruiters

*The new reality: The chances of executive recruit-
ers filling a job that is right for someone, at the
moment they contact them is a little like finding a
needle in a haystack. But, they still are potentially
very important. Here are some thoughts to keep in
mind.*

*T*here's no question that recruiters can be of help to your
career. But, if you send them an unsolicited resume, the
chance of their working on a job that is just right for you at
the moment you contact them is very small. However, you
can improve your odds by using superior materials and by
mailing to larger numbers of the right recruiters.

Executive search firms typically fill positions from $70,000
to $300,000 and up. Many people refer to them as headhunt-
ers, and their assignment is to find qualified candidates
who meet highly specialized criteria.

For the most part they are retained for searches on an
exclusive basis, and they charge their employer clients 30%
to 33% of the annual compensation of the position they are
seeking to fill. To distinguish themselves in their industry,
they are sometimes referred to as "retainer recruiters."

The number of executive job openings they control is
sizable, but still only 9% of the market. Furthermore, on a
national scale, a relatively small number of firms control
much of the business, even though there are upwards of
7,000 recruiters who claim to be active in the field. Certain
recruiters enjoy considerable prestige, often working only
on select, high-level assignments. However, there are also
many very fine smaller firms who specialize in just a single
industry or several industries or disciplines.

On a personal level, recruiters are usually articulate professionals who have a broad knowledge of business. The successful people in the field are generally excellent marketing people themselves.

How do executive recruiters find candidates? Recruiters have a preference for achievers, people who make strong first impressions and who are successfully employed in other firms. These are the individuals who are most presentable to their clients and who are easiest to sell to them.

Their sources for finding people range from directories and articles in the press to their own broad-range contacts and files of resumes. Of course, the preferred relationships with these firms are the ones that begin with their contacting you. Being visible in your industry is the major key to success with recruiters. Being in a hot field or industry can improve things still further.

If you have kept track of the recruiters who have called you in the past, one of the first things you should now do is renew these relationships.

To get results through a mail campaign, a superior summary of your qualifications is essential. Keep in mind that recruiters are "assignment-oriented." They will be focused on filling their active contracts. In most cases, all that will happen is that you will simply be getting into their files.

At the executive level, mailings of 300 or more are common, and should go out at the beginning of your search. A historical arrangement of your background will normally produce the most response. Keep records of all replies from recruiters. Using impressive materials, over a six-week

---

"We review every resume, but the background of the candidate must be right on target for what we're working on. Otherwise, there's not a chance we'll respond."

— Doug Andrews, Executive Recruiter, Clarey and Andrews

period you can expect positive response that will usually range from 1% to 4% — depending on your field, industry, and income level.

If your correspondence fails to supply a phone number that is answered during normal business hours, you will lose many leads. Voice-mail service or an answering machine is a must. Another point to remember is that a second mailing to the same list 10 to 12 weeks later usually produces equal results.

Keep in mind that many large firms are contacted by 50 to 200 job seekers each day. This means there will be instances where a recruiter calls you *months* after the firm first receives your resume.

Regardless, recruiters will be interested primarily in those viewed as marketable, who have blue-chip or high-demand backgrounds, and who have industry knowledge that can quickly help their clients.

You will be most popular with recruiters if you are a person who will explore more attractive situations but who is not too unhappy with his or her current employer. Be honest while pursuing a soft sell. If you are desperate or too available, they will never recommend you to their clients.

One last thought on recruiters. In an interview, Duke Foster of *Korn/Ferry*, often considered the largest search firm with 58 offices worldwide, indicated that every executive resume they receive is scanned, with one exception. In most cases, if there is no indication of current income or range of desired earnings, your material will never find its way into their national and international database, which is maintained in Los Angeles.

And, by the way, when you visit these firms, you had better be good at interviewing or you may have to write a recruiter off for the balance of your career. Remember, the recruiter is measuring not only how well you are qualified... but how well you will sell.

Uncovering the
right recruiters to contact

We provide clients with the recruiters they should contact by screening through databases which cover over 7,000 recruiters. Through these files, we are able to identify various specialists who have the highest probability of being interested in their credentials. Of course, your best prospects will be recruiters with whom you have had a past relationship. Recruiting firms can also be identified in the yellow pages, as well as in published directories.

In summary, recruiters can be very important. However, don't allow more than 10% of your effort to be focused on recruiters. Cover the market with a mailing utilizing superior materials, and consider doing a follow-up mailing 10 weeks later.

9

The Only Way
to Answer Ads

The new reality: Less than 1% of all executive jobs are ever advertised, and the percentage is declining every year. However, there are a few angles that can increase your odds, and there is one key rule you need to follow.

Most estimates place the advertised portion of the executive job market at less than 1% of all openings. What's more, many of the more attractive advertised openings bring 200 or more responses. So obviously, this is an extremely competitive environment. Here are some pointers.

When you start your search, answer all good ads from the last 13 weeks. A percentage of those openings will already be filled, but a number will still be open.

As you identify new ads to answer, delay your response five days. When employers screen a lot of applicants, they begin by discarding any resumes that include anything that will rule the person out. This produces a manageable amount of paperwork, which is then reviewed more carefully.

By the way, did you ever see an ad and feel, *that describes me exactly?* Well, as a general rule, once you have responded, if you have not heard anything after two weeks have passed, you should follow up. If you were a good fit for the job, answering ads twice can work.

A strategy for finding more ads to answer involves the use of what is called downgrading, upgrading, and sidegrading. For example, a company advertising for a CFO might be willing to hire a senior financial type who could move up to CFO. It isn't so much the title they are after, as the skills and talent. That's an example of downgrading.

By the same token, a company advertising for a Director of Manufacturing might be persuaded to hire a VP of Manufacturing, provided someone could persuade the potential employer that such a move would be cost efficient and would offer added capabilities. That's an upgrade.

Ads can also be used as signals of private openings in other areas of the company. If you see a company hiring a number of salespeople, that's a fairly reliable indicator that it is also hiring a few executives in other areas. That's sidegrading.

The number one key to success when answering ads is to use letters alone, rather than a cover letter with a resume. As I mentioned, because employers receive so many resumes, they tend to start by screening out non-qualifiers. This is a critical point. Because resumes provide more facts, they can work against you in some situations.

Make use of strong letters, ones that are targeted at the requirements for success in the position. Of course, there are situations where it is wise to use a resume with a cover letter; however, your resume needs to be right on target for the opening that is advertised.

Stay abreast of the advertised openings you should know about

We subscribe to services which enable us to electronically access ads that appear in dozens of major newspapers throughout the country. When one of our clients begins a job search, we can provide a report on the openings that have appeared nationally over the last 13 weeks. Of course, on your own, you will want to stay abreast of openings that appear in *The Wall Street Journal*, your local paper, and any trade magazines within your field. Remember... identifying ads might do it for you, but any effort you spend here should be a minor part of your total marketing campaign.

10

How to Get Interviews by Direct Mail Marketing

The new reality: Mass mailings don't work. Small custom mailings handled in waves, and combined with proper telemarketing can bring success. However, never assume it can be done with the wrong targets or run-of-the-mill materials.

Some people will tell you that direct mail marketing doesn't work. And, it's true that if you distribute standard cover letters with a resume, or if you use the wrong list, you will be wasting a lot of time and money.

However, highly sophisticated and customized mailings can work very well. It takes persuasive writing, the right targets, telephone follow-up, and adherence to proven rules of direct mail. But considering that your career is at stake, it's worth it.

Every day we are all on the receiving end of direct mail. However bad that junk mail may look to you, the fact is that the ones you see again and again are working; otherwise, the senders wouldn't be wasting money by repeating the process.

Direct mail is a game of testing, revising, and testing some more, until you get the right return for the right dollars. And perhaps the number-one rule in direct mail is that "long copy is the name of the game," because that's what it takes to motivate all of us to action from *unasked-for correspondence.*

The philosophy of direct mail — "timing is everything"

Let's assume your local lawn mower shop wants you to come in and see a new product it is carrying. Also, let's say that you and your next door neighbor are both out cutting your lawns on a brutally hot day. However, your lawn mower keeps stopping and starting, and finally it gives out completely.

Then, the mail carrier arrives at both residences with this long piece of mail that tells you all about a revolutionary new lawn mower, a long explanation of why it's superior to everything else ever manufactured and, guess what, it's available locally. Now, chances are your neighbor will look at the mailing piece for about two seconds and toss it, wondering how anyone could ever read all that material.

Obviously, he isn't in the market for a lawn mower. On the other hand, because the mailing piece has reached you at precisely the right time, it's likely that you will read it quite thoroughly. Perhaps you might be motivated to make a local visit and a purchase!

Now, your position relative to using direct mail is really very similar. Your interest is in reaching the right person who might be in the market for someone like you—right now. No one else counts.

To make direct mail work, you will also need to understand how to use telemarketing in conjunction with direct mail. Of course, very few employers will be needing someone like you the day your material arrives. That's why this is a low-percentage response game. The key is to follow traditional direct mail and follow-up techniques.

Remember, direct-mail enables you to project your best image, avoid initial disclosure of any liabilities, and make contact that is free from competition. What's more, you have a universe of possibilities to contact.

Your priority list
of high probability targets

You need to decide on a selective list of preferred organizations and people in them to contact. Your "priority list" needs to take into consideration the industries for which you are best suited, your preferred locations, and the size of organization to which you would be most appealing.

In the largest organizations, CEOs or senior vice presidents in charge of specific functions are recommended targets. In smaller firms you will need to reach the top executive or owner.

Your next step is to divide your initial list into three parts according to your "best of best," other "prime choices," and those who are really "secondary choices" you might consider. This carefully tailored target list of employers should be added to as you go through your search. Your goal, of course, is to get an interview with the right person in these organizations, whether you do it by networking, telemarketing, or direct mail.

To make it easy to do this with some speed and convenience, taking advantage of the expanding world of computer databases is a must. Literally dozens of databases are available, any of which can save you time.

Keep in mind that all of them will be at least 10% out of date. Typically, you can select organizations by industry, location, and size and then get information such as the company name and address, telephone number, and names of CEOs and their officers by area of specialty.

"As far as direct mail is concerned, you better have the right people to get in touch with or you'll come up with zero."

— Sam Robertson, VP HR, Computer Company

Planning your
direct mail actions

It's important to do your mailing in waves, over a period of time. You'll get your best response by personally calling everyone you have written. Then, each month you need to assess the results and make revisions to your creative materials as you go forward.

Mass mailings rarely work. People who send out thousands of traditional resumes usually get little to nothing in return. Quite frankly, if job hunting were that simple, everyone would just put their resumes in the mail.

Nevertheless, there are mailing firms who advertise, and who will send you copies of resumes that they claim produced fantastic mailing results. Often, these are standard one-page resumes with a one-paragraph cover letter, but the clever marketing approach convinces many that large mass mailings can get them an executive job. *"Caveat Emptor"* or *"let the buyer beware" certainly applies here.*

From our perspective, the key to direct mail success rests with small micro-mailings, using tailored materials for each application, with adjustments made creatively based on the percentage of response (as opposed to the "mass approach," where people often send out standard resumes with a hope and a prayer). Of course, there are certain occupations where you have a limited number of potential employers, for example, musicians, educators, broadcasters, etc. Here, your campaign will be most effective with long-copy letters. Once again, mailings in waves will allow time for selected telephone follow-up.

"I look at the letters and resumes that cross my desk. If something stands out as a fit at the moment, I may respond directly. It's a matter of timing."

— Jim Falletti, Senior VP, Ameritech Corp.

The types of
marketing letters

Keep in mind that when it comes to direct mail, letters can be every bit as important as resumes. You must customize your appeal for each audience. Here are a few pointers that can be helpful.

Cover letters. These should be interesting and brief. Get to the point and make sure they're good.

Letter-resumes. These are stand-alone letters that are not forwarded with a resume. They must provide sufficient "resume-type information" to stimulate interest. Use them whenever you want to fully tailor the description of your credentials, and avoid revealing any liabilities.

Handwritten memos. These are fast and easy to send off, and executives are used to such notes. If you have some superior resumes that are on-target for your different audiences, attaching such notes can work very well.

Benefit letters. Materials that emphasize what you can do — as well as the results you can bring — are ideal. Next best are letters that talk about your previous accomplishments and the results you achieved. Least effective are letters that list your past experience and work history.

Letter structure. The opening should almost always demonstrate your specific interest (knowledge of the firm, its industry, etc.) and explain your reason for writing. The body must convey your qualifications and potential benefits. Our philosophy is to lead off with each person's best selling-points. Then, we enlarge upon them, citing examples when appropriate, and presenting our clients as the answer to a need or problem. The closing should restate interest, confirm the desire for an interview, and say when you will be following up.

The mailing approaches
you can choose from

Now, there are many approaches to the mechanics of direct mail itself. For example, let's assume you are seeking a Vice President of Sales position in a large corporation. Here are some of the direct-mail approaches you might consider taking:

❏ High risk. Sent to people by generic titles, e.g. all SVPs of Sales at Fortune 500 firms. May result in no response.

❏ Slightly better. Sent randomly to many CEOs. Takes great credentials to work.

❏ Much better. Sent to SVP Sales, selected by industry, size, and location. Can be good with follow-up.

❏ Very good. Sent to SVP Sales in industries where you have experience; mention it early, and follow up.

❏ Excellent. Sent to SVP Sales to whom you have spoken. Great if you can get your telemarketing on a roll.

❏ Also Excellent. Sent to SVP Sales where mailing goes out under someone else's letterhead.

❏ Outstanding. Sent to SVP Sales to whom you've been referred by someone, with telephone follow-up.

❏ Best. Sent to SVP Sales whom you have met socially or in business, with follow-up.

"Third-party letters can be very effective if the right person is writing for you. It doesn't need to be a close friend; just make it easy for them to assist. I'd prepare a letter for their signature."

— John Windsor, Former HR Executive, Hoechst Celanese

The essential
direct mail rules

❏ Assembly-line materials don't work. Long copy works best, but letters must be crisp. Keep sentences short. Avoid flowery words. Keep paragraphs to five or six lines. Indent the first line.

❏ If you have industry experience, mention it early!

❏ Use the names of both the firm and the individual in the body of your letter. In most cases don't explain why you are looking.

❏ Persuasive letters "read" just like you "speak." Read your letters out loud to see if they need more work.

❏ Personalize your letters by using "I," "my," or "we." Always be enthusiastic. Everyone prefers people who really want to be associated with him/her.

❏ Commit yourself to a telephone follow-up. Name the date and general time you will call.

❏ Never mention your expected income.

❏ Keep records of all direct mail. Follow-up mailings get 80% of the response of your first mailing.

❏ If you have a strong interest in a large firm, consider sending materials to several top executives in that organization.

❏ Use a standard of quality in your materials that is befitting someone at your level.

Direct mail itself is a low percentage response game. The lower your position objectives, the higher the response. Positive response refers to any favorable inquiry over a four to six-week period. It may be a request for further information, a phone discussion, or a request for an interview.

Here is an example of how direct mail was used in two campaigns. It involved two people simultaneously — the EVP and number-two person in a Fortune 200 pharmaceutical firm and the president of a division of the same firm. Both were terminated because of a merger, and both lived in the New York area.

The EVP was moved into a presidency with a division of another pharmaceutical firm in New York inside of twelve weeks. Fewer than 80 three-page custom letters were circulated within the industry — each of which was followed up by phone.

The other person campaigned for 18 weeks before relocating as CEO of a smaller west coast firm. Seven different mailings of 200 each were involved. The key was the seven different letters that were customized to each group.

Finding the right organizations and people to contact

You can't effectively do direct mail without making use of some good databases. We use them to identify the organizations and people who are the highest-probability targets for being interested in our clients. With 10,000,000 employers out there, finding the right targets, by metropolitan area, by specific industries of interest, and by growth rates, can save weeks of time. As you go through your career search you can also add to your priority list by making the most of a vast number of trade directories.

11

Power Phone Strategies

The new reality: Executives who are "pros" with the phone are the ones who consistently generate the most activity. Getting interviews by phone can be your quickest way to success.

Some people are totally confident in their ability to use the phone. However, 90% of all job seekers are reluctant to do much cold calling. Nevertheless, effective use of the phone is easier than you think. In fact, if you're not experienced at telemarketing yourself, believe it or not, it's a mostly friendly and helpful world out there.

The difference between simply making phone calls and "telemarketing" is very basic. When you telemarket, you have specific goals and you use a standardized procedure for making a larger number of calls.

Basic guidelines
that always apply

❏ Get used to making one call after another. Stand up and you give a power assist to your voice. Do your phone work in batches; you need only one success each time to sustain your morale.

❏ Plan how you will be answering your phone. Prepare answers to the difficult questions you expect. Prepare a 30-second commercial of your best selling-points. Rehearse it, tape it, and critique it.

❏ As you know, one of the best times to reach other executives is before 9:00 A.M. or after 5:00 P.M.

❏ Smile while speaking and your voice will sound pleasant. Be friendly, enthusiastic and positive.

❑ Project a natural, confident tone — as when talking with a friend. Lower your voice and speak slowly. Be prepared for rejection. This is a numbers game.

❑ Recognize that the secretary doesn't know who you are. If you only want information, the boss has no reason to shy away from you. Get the secretary's name and use it. Be confident, positive, and polite. Don't reveal too much of your story. You want to set an appointment, not be interviewed on the phone.

Opening approaches to starting your conversations

The good news approach: *"Mr. Ellis, when I heard about your four quarters of record growth..."* Everyone likes to have good things happen and to hear from others who are enthusiastic about their good fortune.

The third-party approach: *"Bill Regan, a partner with Andersen, thought I should call because of your merger. Do you have a moment?"* If you mention the name of someone who knows the person you're calling, it helps establish rapport, and it works even when they don't know each other.

The specific-reason approach: *"Mr. Franklin, I have a specific reason for calling you. I know something of the processes you use; during the past year, I saved a firm like yours approximately $2,000,000. I would like to share the details with you if you suggest a convenient time."*

The "perhaps-you-can-help-me" approach can be used in just about any situation. *"Hi, Mr. Ellis, I'm Tom Cole. Perhaps you can help me. After reading the recent Fortune article, I wondered if you could refer me to..."*

"The problem for certain executives is that they don't understand that they better get to a state of mind that it's OK to call people." — Frank Reigel, Senior VP, Lockheed

How to handle the people
who screen your calls

❑ Identify yourself with an organization. Use the name of the person who is the "screener." Once identified, people's manners become more personal. Remember, the more expert the screener is, the more potentially valuable that person may be. If you don't get through on your first attempt, suggest a time when you will call back.

❑ When you call back, use the screener's name. If the person is difficult to reach, say: "Since he's hard to reach, would you do me a favor? May I call back at 5:00 P.M. to see if he would be free to speak for a few minutes?"

❑ If you must leave a message, leave one of potential benefit to the person you are calling. Also consider reversing your attempt to speak with the decision-maker by asking for an internal referral to another line manager.

❑ If the screener refers you to the HR department, get the name of the person to whom you will be speaking. Call back later or request a transfer.

❑ Ask two or three penetrating questions about the company's needs. When asked difficult questions, people who don't know the answer are more inclined to refer you to the right person.

❑ After a few days, call back the screener and explain that while the HR staff was helpful, they were not really able to answer the questions you had in mind.

❑ If you encounter the question, "Are you looking for a job?" The answer : *"Yes, I am; do you think you could help me? A friend suggested your firm to me."*

❑ Or, if you encounter, "We don't have any openings at the present time," respond, *"You know I have such a strong interest in the firm, I really believe I could be a great asset. May I tell you why?"*

After you reach the right person, here are some openers

❑ "In your annual report, I read that the company's expanding in the medical products field. That's an area where I could help, and I wanted to share some thoughts. Is there a good time for an appointment?"

❑ "My friend, Tim Ellsworth, suggested that I make a point of contacting you. You may recall from my letter that I have experience in raising capital..."

❑ "Mr. Barker, your company has a tremendous reputation for market-leading products. I'd like very much to share with you how I could contribute to that reputation through my work in Japan."

There's obviously much more to telemarketing than I can address here. If getting on the phone does not come naturally to you, pick up one of the many books on this subject.

How to come up with the people to contact by phone

By sorting through our electronic files, we are able to provide our clients with organizations and people they should consider contacting by phone. This is done in the same way we develop recommended contacts for direct mail. You can supplement your contact list through local directories, phone books, and other guides which cover the metropolitan areas and industries in which you are interested. In summary, make it a point to become a "pro" on the phone. Your confidence will soar, and you'll save an enormous amount of job-search time.

"People tend to give up too easily. I read that we received 1.5 million resumes in one year. But, if people can make calls without being obnoxious, they'll get an interview... sooner or later." — Anonymous Executive, IBM

12

Networking Old Contacts and Building New Ones

The new reality: There's nothing like personal contacts; however, the people who depend on them too much may be in for a long search. Here are some thoughts on making the most of your old contacts, and even building new ones from a zero base.

*I*t wasn't too long ago that if you asked most people about the way they could quickly find a new position, they would tell you that the answer was their connections.

However, in today's environment, when many people must consider either changing careers or industries, the importance of your connections, and your credentials, isn't quite the same.

Nevertheless, there's no substitute for personal contacts who can really be of help. The best way to use them is to never ask directly for a situation in their organization. Of course, most people never get the most out of contacts they may have worked a lifetime to develop.

Have you ever heard a person say, *"I've asked all of my friends to be on the lookout"*? They honestly believe they've done everything they can to get help. If they thought about it, they would realize that they've probably approached these friends on a very general basis and asked a favor which is next to impossible. They say, *"Let me know if you hear of anything, Joe."* Joe, of course, will keep his friend in mind, but probably only for a very short time. Five minutes later, Joe is back to his routine, and his friend is forgotten.

However, the fact remains that Joe was probably willing and might have been able to help. How do you avoid the same mistake? One answer is to make your request sound important, but to also make sure your communication is a pleasant experience for them.

Remember, people are far more likely to respond if you make it easy for them to assist you. For example, you might ask a past associate if he knows of any top executives among some growth companies you have identified. Or you could ask a financial executive to review recent financial job openings with you and request permission to use his/her name in a cover letter.

On the other hand, you could ask a top person at a former customer to arrange letters of introduction to companies in his field. Then offer to draft a letter. Or, if you know someone in human resources, you could see if he would help by lending his name for contacting recruiters. Let him know the jobs that interest you, the firms that have appeal, and just what you want him to do. The best way to use these people as a source of referrals is to ask their permission to possibly use them as a reference.

An example of a
perfect endorsement

Consider the story of Phil. His boss kept telling him he was worth more, but the firm was losing money. When Phil heard that the company was to be sold, he felt his $100,000 salary was $30,000 less than it should be.

We helped make him aware of the power of his contacts. Would his boss, a good friend, be a good reference? And did the boss feel bad about paying him less than he was worth? Absolutely! Could Phil ask him to be a reference, and would he raise him to a level of $130,000 in return for his staying the last two months? That's what Phil asked for and got!

Now, the boss had a friend who was a partner in an accounting firm. Phil asked his boss if he would approach his friend as a reference. Together, they visited over lunch. Guess what? He was happy to act as a second reference. In the same way, Phil developed a third reference, his own brother-in-law.

When he launched a campaign, he had a good interview with the president of a privately-owned company. A conservative man, the president asked for three people who could speak about him. Phil immediately recontacted everyone, so they were ready. After his boss had given him a glowing reference, the president mentioned that he was still uncertain. When the second person (the boss's friend) was called, he said that in the right situation Phil could help save a million dollars in taxes and cost reductions. He also repositioned Phil, in the eyes of this president, to a broader-based financial executive.

Next, Phil's third supporter endorsed what the others said and added a few points. Within days, he got a call from the president, and guess what? His message was, *"Phil, what will it take to get you?"* Phil ended up with a position as VP finance at $145,000.

How to set up
your references

Most of the time, important references will be the people you reported to in the past, the person you currently report to or their superiors, and, on rare occasions, the people who worked for you. Choose the highest level reference, as long as you get an enthusiastic endorsement, and avoid people who don't communicate well. They should be people who have no hesitation in making strong statements about you. Even though you may never have worked for them, all types of respected people might be of help.

In most cases, three references will suffice. Be sure to prepare your references with care. Let them know that you have a high regard for their opinions; this will reinforce the positive chemistry between the two of you and make them want to do their best for you. Don't forget that even good personal contacts will know only part of your background. Make sure that they learn the full story.

In the vast majority of situations, you will provide the names of your references rather than presenting letters of recommendation. In the nonprofit, academic, and government areas, however, it is traditional to collect written recommendations. These endorsements are frequently required in politically sensitive situations.

Another point is that some of your contacts are likely to be your best sources of referrals to employers. When you've really polished your materials, leave them some resumes, and be sure to reassure them that you will not abuse the use of their names. After calling your contacts, send a brief note that shows your appreciation and summarize a few positive

---

"What your references say is very important, but the enthusiasm and conviction they project is even more important!"
— Charles Daniels, Management Psychologist

things they can say about you. You can even prepare a list of questions that employers might ask and suggest some answers for them. By the way, be sure to let your contacts know as soon as you have used their name, and ask them to let you know when they have been contacted. This is important because employers will sometimes ask them for someone else who is familiar with your performance.

When checking, people may want to discuss your management style, ethics, work habits, people skills, etc., in addition to confirming dates and incomes. Assume that employers will want to check with your past superiors. Track these people down for at least the last three jobs or ten years. Don't be reluctant, even if you have not bothered to keep in touch. People like to learn what is happening to others.

In the case of people who have moved into top management, references from any but the last one or two positions are rarely needed. Let the employer know that you need to keep your activity confidential. This lets them know you have a worthwhile position to protect.

If you have worked in one company for a long time, contact former employees or bosses who have left your company and ask them to be references. If appropriate, consider using customers, suppliers, or trade group contacts.

Job seekers often struggle with concerns about bad or questionable endorsements. It's long been said that bad references won't hurt as much as the good ones that turn out to be poor. If someone is apt to give you a less-than-glowing recommendation, bring it out in the interview and then

---

"We never hire someone at the senior level without checking references. It's taken for granted, that we'll ask to see a copy of their W2 or income tax."

— Ralph Gradishar, Division CFO, Cosmetics Firm

supply enough people to offset it. For example, if the inter-viewer asks to speak with someone who will be question-able, defuse the situation by explaining that you had differences of opinion on some managerial styles. Remain totally objective and unemotional, and never imply nega-tives about that person.

Also, you might have a friend do a mock reference check to find out what is being said. If the person is neutral, don't hesitate to ask the person to furnish more positive informa-tion. As a last resort, you may have to imply that you will seek a legal remedy.

How to network
strangers and influentials

Numerous articles have said that many people have been networked to death. However, the amazing thing is that it still works very well. You need finesse, you need to be very clear about your objectives, and you need to use your time extremely well. By networking effectively, your phone pres-ence, personality, and follow-through can substitute for precisely the right experience. Networking works because every organization experiences turnover — and a great deal more of it than they like to admit. In addition, recruit-ing is very expensive.

Networking within an industry where you have experi-ence or interests and networking efforts directed to influen-tial people are where you want to concentrate. Governors, congressional representatives, state senators, and other politicians can be excellent sources for referrals. The same is true for prominent doctors and lawyers who speak with many people during the course of each day. Clergy, CPAs, hospital trustees, directors of chambers of commerce or other civic groups, members of industrial development boards, investment bankers, insurance brokers, and many others also fall into this category.

Another option is to expand your networking effectiveness through business activities. Here you simply have to increase your visibility. You can expand your business network by visiting places patronized by those in your field, or attending seminars, parties, and supplier meetings.

Trade shows have long been an efficient medium for developing contacts. In one location, you usually have dozens of people assembled, and all of them are there because they want to talk to people. Still others have had success by networking through associations. Many professional organizations, alumni, and trade associations act as intermediaries between job hunters and employers. The executive directors of associations, chambers of commerce, and fraternal organizations or Jaycees usually have many "lines" into their communities. They know where growth is occurring.

Professional groups also fund and manage business magazines, journals, newsletters, membership lists, industry directories, and trade show catalogs. The editors at these journals can be influential contacts.

Some everyday networking guidelines

Once you've made contact, one key to successful networking lies in asking the right questions. When probing for information from someone you don't know well, keep the questions broad, and related to the industry. Naturally, you want to know about trends in any business in which you might want to work. They can facilitate the kind of shoptalk shared at a trade conference. Here are some sample questions you might consider asking for general information:

"Am I responsive to others who network me? Very much so. Who knows when I may be in the same position."

— Fortune 500, VP Public Relations

What are the long-term trends in your industry? With those trends in mind, what skills are companies likely to be looking for in new executives? What are some good sources of additional information, either articles and reports, or people to talk to? Who are the active recruiters in the industry? What are the fastest growing areas of the business?

When your contact is interested enough to concentrate on your career needs, obviously different questions are appropriate. There are many common errors that people make while networking. Here are some points to remember.

❑ Networking is part of the "job" of looking for a job. List people you want to see, and find a way to get through. Getting through isn't the victory; that comes only after you've completed a successful interview.

❑ Be prepared. Know what strengths to get across.

❑ Talk with people wherever you go. Let people know that you are thinking about a new opportunity. Most people understand when they're "being networked" so you should never try to fool them.

❑ Keep your interviews brief. Ask for ten-minute appointments. Leave every meeting with several new names and make note of the names of secretaries. Send a thank you note after your interview.

❑ Exchange business cards with everyone you meet.

In summary, there's nothing like personal contacts; however, before you approach them, make sure that your goals are clear and your materials are just right. Ask them to be a reference, and, of course, for referrals, and make it as easy as possible for them to help.

"Absolutely the best way for executives to find jobs is to network with as many other executives as possible."

— Bill Mattarick, VP HR, TRW, Inc.

13

How to Get an Employer to Create a Job for You

The new reality: Knowing how to get a job created needs to be one of your capabilities. Let's face it, everybody's looking for talent if they have benefits to bring them. With a little initiative, many people have created their own destiny.

You can get offers, even if no job openings are said to exist. You simply need to present yourself as a solution to a problem. The "create a job" approach is for people who want a job tailored to their best abilities, or who may have difficulty winning offers through other means.

A few examples might include a person who can develop new products for a company, a sales executive with contacts in particular markets, or a general manager who can start up a division in a specific industry.

The "create a job" approach should also be considered by anyone who may have difficulty winning offers through other means. This includes those with a narrow market; people who wish to change industries; or those who have been unemployed for a while or who want to stay in a specific geographic or industry area. In these situations, to win the job you want, you may have to create it by making an employer aware of your ability to make contributions.

Keep in mind this simple thought. Employers hire people whenever they are persuaded that the benefit of having them on board outweighs the dollar cost. The following pages will give you some guiding principles as you consider this approach.

Creating a job — Principle #1
Target smaller firms and reach people in authority

The first principle to understand is that to have your best chance at creating a job, your highest-probability targets are likely to be small to medium-sized companies. This includes firms that are growing rapidly, bringing out new products, forming new divisions, acquiring other companies, or reorganizing.

These are the firms that need good people, often from other industries. They are free to move quickly. Large corporations are the least likely to respond to this approach. Budgets are usually allocated far in advance, and hiring practices tend to be relatively slow and methodical.

Of course, there are exceptions. All you need to do is assess your talents and contact the firms most likely to need you, regardless of their size or stability. And if you know a market well or have talents in a particular function, just consider the industries where they would apply.

Of course, you must reach people in authority, the appropriate high-level people in each firm you contact. For example, you must be able to communicate directly with the person you would most likely work for, or that person's boss. In small and medium-sized companies, this is normally someone at or near the top. Entrepreneurs, of course, are ideal for contacting in this regard.

"I created most of my positions. When I moved to my senior VP position, I had gone to an annual meeting and met with a friend. The next thing I knew they found a role for me. Now I run the firm." — Anonymity requested

Creating a job — Principle #2
Use a benefit proposition

Your benefit proposition must be an accurate, concise, and easily understood description of what you can do. Your message has to hold the promise of tangible value on a scale large enough to warrant an investment in you. In that initial communication, you will also need to establish your credentials. Mention specific results you achieved in the past. They are the best indicators of what you can do in the future. By the way, achievements don't have to be large, but they do have to be significant.

One key point to remember is that if you have an exciting idea to communicate, it may help if you can show how someone else has already used that idea successfully. Dealing with opportunities is a key job for many executives. Most don't have enough time in the day and are predisposed to positive news from people who can help them. They will want to believe your message, so all you need do is make sure you provide positive reinforcement.

By the way, you can get your message across by phone or with a letter. Either way, make sure your "benefit position" is clear, easy to measure, and significant; and be prepared to establish your credentials quickly.

"Some years ago, I hired a coach from a little-known California university. The only reason I saw him was that he wrote such a good letter outlining what he thought he could do for us." — Owner, NFL football team

Creating a job — Principle # 3
Identify their problems, their needs, and their vision

Your initial communication held out the promise of a major benefit. So, when you get the interview, you need to be ready. What are your ideas? What makes you confident they'll work? Do you understand the company's problems and opportunities? Address these areas, but always remember to convey humility. For example, you might say:

"I hope you didn't find my letter too presumptuous. No doubt you've already given a lot of consideration to these areas." Or... "I'm sure you've talked to many people who thought they knew your business better than you do. I don't mean to come across that way. I have a number of ideas, but let me first pay you the courtesy of listening to your opinion on these areas."

Comments like these set the stage for a cordial exchange of ideas. They can allow you to do the three things you need to accomplish in your first meeting: learn what the employer really wants; build rapport; and focus the employer's attention on areas where you can help.

Your first goal is to find out how the employer views the problem. What are the key challenges? What is the "hot button?" Where are the priorities? What attempts have been made in the past? How much progress has been made?

Make sure you maintain a balanced conversation. Ask questions and make positive comments in response to the interviewer's remarks. Most important, try to get the employer to share his innermost thoughts and his vision for the organization. Only when he starts to think about this and the significant achievements he might realize, would he consider the possibility of creating a job. State that you would like to give things some further thought and then clarify the benefits you might bring to the situation. Show your enthusiasm and get agreement that a second interview would be worthwhile.

Creating a job — Principle # 4
Stir the employer's imagination

In your second interview you must reinforce your value by drawing an unusually clear picture of the benefits you can bring. Then you need to build enough enthusiasm to get an offer or be asked to speak with others.

The employer should begin to anticipate specific benefits and be able to relate them directly to your talents. The entire focus of the conversation should be on the future, with the employer picturing a company already benefitting from your contributions.

A dry recitation of proposed improvements won't be enough. You will have to convey enthusiasm and create a sense of excitement. To do this you will have to refine your thinking, clearly identifying those areas the employer sees as most important. For each of them, be ready to discuss general approaches you would take to reinforce the notion that you will succeed.

Your best way to do this is to tell stories about your past achievements. If you build sufficient enthusiasm, the employer may conclude the meeting with a statement that he'd like to create a job for you. Or, he may ask you to meet with others in the company. If that happens, take the opportunity to build additional enthusiasm with every member of the team.

"It was very rare. But any decision we made to create a job was as much emotional as it was intellectual."

— Pete Sullivan, Former VP, AT&T

Creating a job — Principle #5
Consider the report option

If you're not getting interest, you might make an offer to study the situation in more detail, perhaps to observe the company's operations or talk to knowledgeable outsiders, and to come back with a written report. The purpose? To make the entire subject more significant in their mind.

The report should discuss the areas where you would make contributions. For each area, you would want to point out how you would proceed, demonstrating carefully the near-term benefits for the company. If you get interesting input from outsiders or cite examples that support your points, it will make your presentation more compelling.

If you try the report option, stage it properly. Let the employer think it's important and ask for adequate time to present your findings. Your report, of course, would include a recommendation that a job be created.

In summary, top management in most companies are well aware of the expenses involved in recruiting. When someone exceptional comes to their attention, many can act rapidly to create a job situation. They develop a new position or shift someone of lesser talent to make room. Every day, people win positions created this way. You can too.

"It is the same principle used by consultants, ad agencies, and top sales producers when they want to stimulate a company to action. The very act of a study, and the presentation of a report following it, builds an aura of importance."

— Glenn Scott, Sr. VP, Princeton/Masters

14

A Plan for
Getting Interviews

*The new reality: Job hunting is a numbers game,
and a lot of contacts are needed to generate the
right number of interviews. However, most people
proceed by trial and error. Having a strategic plan
will save you a lot of time and money.*

We believe in developing action plans for getting our
clients interviews. Following an action plan enables them to
job hunt with far less strain, confusion, or worry, and keeps
them on track. Without one, most people take haphazard
actions, hoping that they'll get the results they want.

Today, following a plan makes a lot of sense for anyone
who is serious about job hunting. It will help you approach
job-hunting actions systematically and will produce far better
results. The concept is simple. There are no gimmicks involved. Rather, it is a process for deciding on the number of
interviews people want to generate, then backing into a
series of job hunting actions that will yield that number of
interviews.

Let's review the key elements
in any marketing effort

Consider for a moment how products are successfully
sold. In most cases, a marketing plan is followed. The starting point is to *understand* all of the vital product information. As I've already discussed, people have to dig deep to
understand what they have to offer the market.

Next, each product must be *positioned* correctly. This
means going after the right career and industry. You seldom
see a product that claims it can do everything for anyone.

Then, you must have the marketing tools to *promote* your product. For executives, this means the resumes and letters, the promotional materials you are likely to require. Like advertising, they should all be developed in advance.

Of course, products need be *priced* right so they will sell. While your income potential will ultimately be determined by supply and demand, your negotiation strategy should be determined at the outset.

When a product is ready to go, it needs to reach the market with the right *distribution*. How will you get your message out, and where will it go? How will you come up with the right leads, contacts, and openings? What are the channels for putting your credentials into the marketplace?

Your action plan
for getting interviews

As you approach your plan, you will need to first decide on the priority you will give your campaign. If you are out of work, you need to design an aggressive campaign — one that might potentially produce more activity than you really need. Any plan requires a timetable. For most executives, we recommend a 13-week schedule. If it ends up taking longer, that's okay, but start by thinking that you want to reach your goal within this period.

Again, job hunting is a numbers game. The more good contacts you make, the more good opportunities that will come your way. We establish action plans by deciding on the number of situations a client would like to explore. For example, someone might wish to explore at least a dozen situations, which, if achieved, might reasonably yield a couple of offers over a 13-week period.

"The less-aggressive executive job seeker has a disadvantage of major proportions. Aggressiveness equals getting discovered." — Ralph Dieckman, Executive Recruiter

To develop that activity, this hypothetical executive might require a plan with a goal of getting two interviews from six of the following seven channels: (1) from answering ads; (2) from contacting recruiters; (3) through pyramiding personal contacts; (4) through networking influential people; (5) through emerging situations identified in the press; (6) through telemarketing to employers on a direct basis; and (7) from micro-mailings to potential employers of interest.

As you implement your plan, you will need to regularly take stock of your progress. For example, are you keeping up with the plan? Are you getting positive feedback on your materials? Are your goals realistic? Is it time for some fine-tuning or adjustments?

If you don't see yourself zeroing in on the right offer, reevaluate your materials or modify your plan. As long as your goal remains unchanged and you remain committed to reaching it, determination and effort are the keys that will ultimately get you there.

To recap, our philosophy includes developing a customized action plan for every client that we assist. A complete track for running their search, it saves our clients time and money, and can dramatically speed their campaign. So follow a plan that is carefully strategized and that addresses what you should do, week by week. Do it right, and the net result will be that you'll get the right new job in less than half the time.

15

Your Most Important Interviewing Strategy

The new reality: With more executives to choose from, employers are increasingly more selective. Your number one interviewing strategy is to build personal chemistry every step of the way.

Getting the right interviews is only half the battle. Let's now discuss just how you can stack the odds in your favor... converting interviews into offers at a higher rate than average. As a general rule, most people require ten or more situations to look into to develop a single offer. If you want to do better, your starting point is to have an interviewing game plan — one in which you conscientiously work at building personal chemistry at all times.

I'm always amazed at how many people treat interviews as just conversations, while others treat them simply as sessions during which they have to answer questions. These things may happen, but an interview that turns into an offer involves far more. Last year there were far more than 100 million interviews. Think about it! What's more, no two were the same. So how do you prepare? Our philosophy is that you do it the same way you would prepare for a sports contest; there are millions of them and none are the same.

In either an interview or a sports contest, you can't plan precisely how things will go, but you can have a game plan. That means knowing the points you want to touch on, the pace you want to maintain, and the questions you want to raise if things are going slowly. Interviewing, of course, is a selling situation. But it's not only what you say that is important. Interviewing involves the exchange of information and the building of personal chemistry.

Building chemistry — Rule #1
Research the company
and getting the office staff on your side

This leads us to your first step for building chemistry, and it involves researching the company in advance. Did you ever meet a person for the first time who knew a lot about you? It takes you by surprise, doesn't it? It's a great way to make a positive first impression.

Many people have built successful businesses that way. One friend of mine, an attorney, attributes his success to the research he does ahead of time. Four out of every five of his clients tell him that he wins their business because he knows a lot more about them than anyone else does.

When you arrange or confirm an appointment, be sure to use the opportunity to gather more information. Many people have been able to get job descriptions, organization charts, and brochures ahead of time simply by requesting them over the phone. That will help prepare you to be able to build better chemistry in your interview.

Building chemistry with the front-office staff can also make a difference. Can you guess what percent of executives say their secretaries influence them? What do you think? One-third? Half? Well, about two-thirds of them do.

Here's how this might affect you. Not too long ago, I was interrupted by Hattie, who stated that Mr. Baxter had arrived for his two o'clock interview. I had forgotten about the appointment, and it was a busy day. I immediately asked, "What do you think of him, Hattie?" She didn't say a word. She just gave a thumbs-down signal. That was the end for poor Baxter. So please be attentive to the secretary and others who work up front, and have a conversation that gives you information that will help in the interview. You may find, as many people have, that when you go out of your way to be respectful to them, they will often go out of their way to help you.

Building chemistry — Rule #2
Project the right image and attitude

Building chemistry is also about attitude and image. My psychologist friends tell me that the way we expect to be treated affects the way we are treated. So build positive expectations about every interview.

Of course, when we are on the hiring end, as employers, many of us reach a negative decision in the first five minutes of an interview. Why? Well, if you have the credentials, you've either established a good initial impression or you haven't. And what determines this personal chemistry?

People silently react to the image you project, your posture and body language, the things you say about any subject at all, and the way you answer questions. So consider the kind of image you project. After all, each of us is continually projecting some kind of image. It isn't just physical image or dress either, although your appearance speaks before you say a word. It's also a matter of attitude, interest, enthusiasm, and whether you come across as a person who is honest, loyal, and in good health.

We tell our clients to check their image before they ever get to the interview, but they shouldn't be too kind to themselves. You might go to someone who is not really close to you and ask them what kind of an attitude they think you project. Ask for their honest opinion of your appearance, eye contact, and mannerisms. Listen to what they have to say; then check out the same things with someone on your side. Somewhere between the two, there will be an accurate picture, and if anything needs to be worked on, do it.

"Nothing is ultimately more important than personal chemistry. When we got down to a few candidates, competency would rarely be the issue."

— Linc Ward, former VP & GM, Pacific Bell

Building chemistry — Rule #3
Compliment others without overdoing it

Do you like receiving compliments? Do you think other people do? You bet they do! So before the interview, read or talk to people about the company and uncover some good things to say. Somewhere in those first few minutes, find the opportunity to let the interviewer know that you heard good things.

This will show that you know something about the company, and it's also what we call a "third-party compliment," where you are passing on the good news that you heard from others. You can compliment their facilities, people, products, advertising, public relations, or many other things.

However, whatever you do, be specific. Don't just say that people you know are impressed by the product. Talk about "why" they are impressed. Maybe it's that new product they added, or the reliability of their products. All of us like to hear about how our products have pleased customers. By giving details, you show that you have given the subject some thought and that your compliment is not just empty flattery.

"This may sound extremely basic. We're a 'shirt-sleeves' company, but our executive selection process is heavy on image and attitude. Surprisingly, a lot of executives miss the cut."

— Parker Tynen, VP Sales, Microchip Company

Building chemistry — Rule #4
Establish rapport as you answer questions

The way you answer questions has more to do with building positive chemistry than with what you say. For example, suppose you get the old standby, the number one question in the world of interviewing: "Tell me about yourself." Many interviews include a form of that question.

You'll want to answer, but chances are you're not sure what they want to hear. You could start out by talking about the kind of person you are and some of your attributes, but that may not be what the interviewer is interested in. Faced with such a dilemma, a safe way out is to self-qualify your answer:

"Certainly, Charles, I'd be happy to tell you about myself, and I'm sure you are interested in my work experience. I'll focus on the past few years and how they relate to this position. I can start with my most recent experience and work backwards if you like."

When you self-qualify like that, you give the interviewer plenty of opportunity to respond, and to direct the conversation toward some other area, if that's not what he or she is really interested in. That way, you can avoid talking for ten minutes about the wrong things.

You will also want to answer questions with good, action-oriented stories. If you fail to tell a story, do you think the interviewer will remember the conversation? Don't count on it. People don't remember answers to questions or concepts. What people remember and what impresses most of them are stories — good stories — action-oriented stories.

When you answer questions, remember to gear your comments to potential contributions relative to sales, profits, cost reduction, efficiency, innovations, quality improvement, etc. When there is a silence, have questions about the field for which you have answers. Create an opportunity to demonstrate knowledge. Being prepared builds confidence and allows you to be more spontaneous. Always maintain eye contact and establish your sincerity and integrity.

When you encounter difficult questions, one way to handle them is with the "U-turn" technique. For example, let's say an interviewer says: "You look very impressive on paper, Carol. If you're this good, you ought to be able to solve all of our problems. Tell me, why should we hire you?"

Now, of course, you know the person doesn't believe you're that good. However, if you begin to talk about why they should hire you, you run the real risk of going on at length about all the wrong things. With the "U-turn" technique, you don't give an answer. Instead, you turn the question around in a way that acknowledges the status of the interviewer and maybe even pays an indirect compliment. Your comment might go something like this:

"I have a lot of experience I believe this firm could use. But it would be presumptuous of me to tell you what you need before I've even shown the courtesy of listening to what you think the priorities are. If you'd be kind enough to share some of your thoughts on these priorities, perhaps I could give a more intelligent answer."

"After-dinner speakers know it, coaches, motivators, and preachers know it. Stories are the best way to make a point. So why not avoid the simple 'yes' answer and have stories ready to make your best points."

Bob Schrier, Managing Dir., Princeton/Masters Southern CA

Building chemistry — Rule #5
Keep rapport as you find out what they want

The next area you need to look at has to do with the question of how you find what the interviewer really wants. Well, sometimes interviewers will get directly to the point and tell you exactly what they are looking for. That makes it easy. Put your listening ability to work. One of the easiest ways to impress people is to ask intelligent and penetrating questions about the firm and the position.

Find out what happened to the last person in the job. Ask the interviewer about his experiences and that of his superiors. If a situation stalls, raise questions by simply asking what? when? where? why? and how? Find out to whom the position reports and how long that person has been in the job. Pinpoint the authority that goes with the job, and find out what they expect you to accomplish in the first six months.

You could ask a simple question such as, "What would be the biggest challenge I would face?" If the interviewer has some reservations, ask a question that is likely to bring them out. Don't forget — you're better off knowing their concerns so that you can deal with them.

Most importantly, find out how the interviewer sees the problem, what the expectations are, and what progress has been made. When you do this, you're learning what the unwritten requirements of the job are.

Let's assume that you've asked the right kinds of questions and done enough listening. Now you know what they want. It's time to let them know you have what they want, and you need to build chemistry as you do it. To create this rapport calls for advance preparation. Ideally, at this stage you should have your own two-minute interviewing commercial ready to go. Again, the purpose is to let them know you have what they want!

Now it's time to determine if you want the job, and you need to keep building chemistry while you do it. One way to do this is to verbalize a positive summary of the meeting, pointing out your enthusiasm about the job. After the summary, ask a question that will generate feedback:

"In your opinion, are my skills and strengths as closely matched to your needs as I think they are? How can we pursue our interests further?"

If you can build chemistry, as well as let the interviewer know what you want, your success may come down to projecting the right image. You want to be looking good and feeling confident, so be sure to dress well and try to get in the best shape you can. When you have a game plan for building chemistry, you will project confidence from knowing what and how to communicate and being ready to do it.

When we manage a campaign, we feel that having a game plan for interviewing is very important. For each client, we advise them on what to say, or omit, in interviews. We also suggest answers for the difficult questions they may be asked, and recommend questions to raise which help control the pace of each interview. Quite often, we do short video interview training sessions to help get them better prepared. Of most importance, we make sure that each person gets used to concentrating on building chemistry at all times.

In summary, employers need to feel that you are a quality person, and hopefully, exactly what they are looking for. However, thousands of job campaigns have produced convincing evidence that jobs at all levels are ultimately won by those who simply establish the best personal chemistry.

"When it comes to executives, companies make their decisions based on the 'fit' — technical, cultural, and personal."
— Jack Bourque, Management Recruiters

16

How to Handle Any
Stressful Interview Questions

The new reality: With today's competition, if you fumble or stumble... there are too many others that every employer can turn to. So, why play it by ear when you are thrown some objections? Here's an easy process to follow that will work every time.

*T*he second key to becoming great at high-level interviewing is to handle whatever objections may come up — and to do it in a way that is comfortable for you. Many of us are more conscious of our liabilities than our strengths. When confronted with a liability, we may become defensive, argumentative, or worst of all, acquiescent.

As mentioned, when faced with objections, the tendency is to become defensive. However, no one sells anything to people while they are arguing with them. You need to have a valid answer when an objection is raised, but jumping to the answer may seem defensive. To avoid that trap you can use a simple process called ARTS. It can help you handle a problem question in a comfortable and effective manner. The letters stand for the following:

> *A — Acknowledge the objection*
> *R — Redirect the person's concern*
> *T — Test to be sure you've removed the concern*
> *S — Use a story to make your point*

Whenever someone raises an objection, the tension level rises. What you want to achieve in step one is to reduce the tension level.

A — Acknowledge the objection.

Here's an example: *"I can understand your concern. It is certainly something we should discuss, and I would like to address it directly for you."* Or... *"You're very perceptive, and you've raised an interesting point. It deserves some frank discussion, and I'd like to address it for you."* The phrases you might use are not so important. Instead, it's the feeling you impart. You haven't gotten flustered. You have acted in a friendly and reassuring way; it's clear that you feel secure about your abilities in the area under question.

R — Redirect their concern.

Going further, here is an example of redirecting the person's concern: *"What qualities are you looking for in an ideal candidate that prompted you to bring this up?"*

Let's say the interviewer raised the objection that your experience was in a different industry. Now, you can't do too much about the fact that your experience was in a different industry, but you probably can show that you are someone who contributes quickly, so that is where you want to direct the conversation.

For example, *"When you raise that question, I understand that you want to be sure the person you put in this job is someone who will contribute quickly. Isn't that it?"* The interviewer will reaffirm that you are indeed correct. As you can see, with just a little thought it is very easy to refocus the conversation toward the positive qualities that are really on the interviewer's mind.

"Most people think interviewing is a natural skill. That's why many people aren't good and never get better."

— Jim Moberg, Executive, Pacific Telesis

T — Use a testing question to see if you removed their concern.

Here is an example of asking a testing question: *"If I could show that I could contribute quickly, even when it comes to learning a great deal of new information, would that help?"* After you get a positive response, you have the option of going directly to your answer, or you can introduce one of your key strengths. You might say: *"If I could show you that I work well under pressure, might that ease your concern somewhat?"*

S — Use a supporting story to confirm your point.

The final thing to do is to use a supporting story as part of your answer, ending it with a feedback question that will keep the conversation positive. Remember, what really counts is the fact that you did not get flustered. Instead, you had a friendly exchange in which you built positive feelings.

If you've done it right, interviewers won't be all that concerned about whether your answer is exactly correct. Instead, they'll be thinking, *"This person handled that situation very well."* Learn how to use this process, and for every concern, you should have your answer ready.

To recap, the second key to interviewing success rests with your ability to handle whatever objections may come up and to do it in a way that is comfortable for you. Get used to the simple process just outlined, and you will be amazed at how effective you will be.

17

Negotiation:
Five Rules for Success

The new reality: An awful lot of people are happy just to get an offer. But, it's easy to do much more. Negotiation can be comfortable and predictable. The key is quite simple. Be prepared and always follow these five negotiation rules.

Negotiation — Rule #1
Always appear sincere and reasonable

*I*n the job search situation, intimidation and attack strategies have no value. One-upmanship can cost you the job. Here you're setting the tone for your long-term relationship.

In fact, most people don't like "negotiation" because they associate it with confrontation, being tough and role playing, something that does not come naturally. The best negotiators are very prepared but avoid anything that might cause irritation. Follow the best negotiators and make sure to be sincere and reasonable... never cold or calculating.

Negotiation — Rule #2
Avoid discussions about money

You need to avoid the lessons we see others learning every day. Here's an example. One client was a general manager with Exxon, earning a substantial income, but wanting to win a new job at a 15% increase. After two meetings, the CEO said, *"Bill, we'd like to have you join us, and I'd like to work out something attractive for you. What have you been used to earning at Exxon?"* At that point, having been encouraged, Bill explained his present income. To make a long story short, he accepted a position at a nice increase. However, he later found out that the last person had been paid 40% more, and that the company expected to match it. Now, the moral is simply that you should never negotiate based on where you've been. Negotiation is like poker. Don't lay your earnings on the table!

Premature discussions about money can be a real deal breaker. Besides, the more enthusiastic an employer becomes about you, the more likely he'll be willing to pay more. Sometimes an interviewer will begin like this: "Jim, before we get started, I'd like to know how much money you are looking for." Here is a possible response.

"Charles, I could talk more intelligently about my circumstances after I know a bit more about the job and the contribution that's possible. Will this job have line responsibilities?" Or, "Charles, I would not take your time if I did not have a fairly good idea of the range you could pay. If we can agree that my experience fits your needs, I doubt we'll have a problem on compensation. My concern is whether your needs call for someone with my background, although I've heard you're entering a number of new markets."

Once again, the U-turn strategy can help you here. Here's how it works:

"For my part, I am most interested in the situation and the people I will work with, the company and my role in the overall effort. And while money is important, I'm not locked into a specific figure because of these considerations."

Using this approach, you remain gracious and friendly while avoiding a direct answer. If an interviewer persists about how much you earned, here is one possible response:

"I would rather avoid discussing compensation until later on. Challenge is most important to me, and I would like to talk money after I know you want me for the job. Is that agreeable to you?" If all else fails, give a range surrounding your estimate of what the job pays.

Negotiation — Rule #3
Express vulnerability, and question, never demand

Let the firm know that accepting the job as offered would cause you difficulties. This plays to the employer's desire to make sure you are happy, so you can devote your full energies to the job. For example, you can be flattered by the offer, but say that you may have to sacrifice your lifestyle, and disappoint your family in order to afford the job:

"I love the job and really want to join with you, but we'd have difficulty making ends meet. Is there a chance you could go a little higher?"

Questioning, rather than demanding, is the rule. The best negotiators persuade others through questions. This gives them the information they need to put themselves in control. It also gives them time to think and never has them putting all their cards on the table.

Good negotiators will not say, "I do not agree with you because..." Rather, they will say, "Charles, you do make a good point, but I wonder if there is room for another view." They would never say, "That would not be any good for me." Instead, they might say, "Charles, could you tell me how you think this would work for me?" Then they will follow up with questions, so the employer can discover that the proposal is not quite enough. And that is your goal: to let employers discover for themselves the validity of your request. If your questions lead them to discover they were wrong, they will be more disposed to changing the terms.

"Our offers always have room if an executive we want is good at negotiation. But if they're only earning $75,000 and looking for $150,000, they shouldn't waste their time."

— Carol Ritenhour, Executive Recruiter, Major Food Company

Negotiation — Rule #4
Never commit when you get an offer.
Suggest alternatives in your next meeting

When offered a job, take the opportunity to praise the company and explain that you need some time to consider it.

"Charles, I am pleased you made me an offer. This is an outstanding firm, and the position has great promise. I am sure you can appreciate that I would like some time to give it further consideration. It would not present any problem, would it, if I were to get back to you tomorrow?"

When you call back, after opening with one or two positive statements, consider raising the possibility of redefining the job. Your conversation might go something like this:

"Charles, with children entering college, I had done some planning based on an income that was $10,000 higher. Would it be possible to take another look at the job specs? For my part, I know that if you could make a modest additional investment, my performance will show you a handsome return. I sincerely hope that we can make some adjustment. Can we take a look at it?"

Of course, if you do not want to redefine the job, but you would still like to raise the salary, you can use the same technique, but show vulnerability, then suggest that a dollar figure be added to the base. Normally, if that figure is within 15% of what you have been offered, the employer will not take offense and will grant you part of it. Of course, asking for more money is a negative, and needs to be balanced by positives. Here is an approach to consider:

"Charles, I cannot tell you how pleased I am. The challenge is obviously there, and I think my experience is perfect for the job. There is one problem, however. You see, one of the main reasons I wanted to make a change was for financial balance. Can you see your way clear to adding $10,000 to the base? It would ease my family situation considerably."

Negotiation — Rule #5
Use your enthusiasm while introducing
other criteria on which to evaluate the offer

If you load maximum enthusiasm into your statements, it becomes nearly impossible for the employer to conclude that you should not be with them. At the same time, follow the principle of introducing other criteria on which to base the offer. This can include the importance of the job to the firm, what you would make with a raise where you are, your total compensation package, what you believe the market is for your background, or other offers you are considering.

In the example that follows, notice how there are no demands, only questions. By your inviting employers to explore the situation with you, they are free to reach their own conclusions about whether their offer is too low. Using this approach, you come across as enthusiastic, sincere, and slightly vulnerable, never as cold, calculating, or aggressively demanding, or as someone who is putting them in a corner. Your comment might be:

"Charles, let me first tell you once again how pleased I am over the offer. I am very positive about the prospect of joining you. I've had the chance now to give it some more thought, and I can only say that my enthusiasm has continued to increase. This is the job I want. It's a situation where I could look forward to staying with the firm for the long-term.

"There is one hurdle that I have to overcome. You see, I've been underpaid for some time, and it has created a financial situation where I need to start earning at a rate which reflects my ability to contribute.

I really don't think most people attempt to negotiate. Frankly, we're in a retail business, and we expect people to negotiate. Sometimes we will change, sometimes we won't."

— Tom Ellis, Senior VP, Major National Retail Organization

"If I stayed where I am, I'd be due for a raise, which would put me close to your offer. In talking with other firms, I've discovered that some of them realize this, and they have mentioned ranges that are 25% higher. Now, I don't want to work for those organizations — I want to work for you. But I do have some pressing financial needs. Perhaps the firm could approve a higher offer. Can we pursue this together?"

Now let's turn to what you should negotiate. Negotiating the nature of the job is your number one goal. Compensation is determined by the responsibilities of the job. So, reshape the job, and the salary range will be higher. For example:

"Charles, there is no doubt that this is a good job. However, based on what you have told me, I believe I could be even more helpful if a few related elements were added. There are three areas where my experience could make a big difference. I'd like to discuss them, so we can see if they could be included in the job description."

You might then go on to talk about the areas where the firm could capitalize on your experience. Believe it or not, reshaping the job can often be that simple. Can you see from the example how the principles were applied? The manner was positive and matter-of-fact, with no confrontation.

"The vast majority of people do negotiate. However, we don't give perks the way we used to. The most common incentive at executive levels is the sign-on bonus. That doesn't throw our compensation and benefit plans out of balance."

— Senior VP, HR, Telecommunications Company

A reminder list of most of
the things you might negotiate

❑ Base salary, commissions, medical and life insurance. You might also try for a signing bonus.

❑ Profit-sharing and pension plans. If you negotiate a share of profits, understand the accounting methods.

❑ Severance payments. A standard agreement covers a year's compensation, and is triggered if the firm lessens your responsibilities or tries to relocate you.

❑ Stock option purchase plans. If you purchase stock at market price, the company may buy an equal amount under your name up to a percentage of your income.

❑ Stock grants. You will most likely be obligated for taxes based upon the market value of shares given.

❑ ISOs (incentive stock options). This is an option to purchase a certain number of shares at market value on a given day, generally exercisable some years away. The primary value of ISOs is that should you eventually buy them, no tax is due on the day you purchase the shares.

❑ Restricted stock units. Stock units are pegged in value; for example, as one share of stock for every five units. The key is when you can convert to cash or shares.

❑ Phantom stock options and stock appreciation rights. Rights to receive the difference in market value between the time granted and value when converted.

❑ Non-qualified stock options. An option to purchase stock below market prices. Tax will be due on the difference between the price at which you exercise your right of purchase and the market value of the stock purchased.

❑ Relocation expenses. This can include house purchase, moving expenses, mortgage rate differential, real estate brokerage, closing costs, cost of bridge loan, trips to look for a home, lodging fees, tuition, installation of materials, and spouse reemployment services.

❑ Other perks can include automobile lease, luncheon, athletic or country club membership, child care, physical exam, disability pay, legal assistance, product discounts, dining room privileges, financial planning assistance, tuition reimbursement, CPA and tax assistance, short-term loans, insurance benefits after termination, special reimbursement for foreign service, outplacement assistance, and deferred compensation.

If you don't have any success in your negotiations, then shift from the "present" and focus instead on "futures," e.g. a review after six months, a better title, an automatic increase after time. These are easier things to get.

Contracts. The following are usually incorporated: the length of the agreement, your specific assignment, your title, location, whom you report to, your compensation and what happens if there is a merger or if you are fired. It should also cover the specific items on the negotiation list that are part of your package. By the way, in most large firms, both signing bonuses and generous severance packages are spreading down the ladder. This is especially true when relocation is involved.

Termination agreement. In most cases, such agreements provide for a minimum severance of six months' salary, relocation expenses, insurance for twelve months, and professional outplacement. Any agreement that you accept should cover all non-legal situations under which an employer may choose to terminate your services.

"We hire a lot of top sales talent. I'm always willing to listen, but I don't respond very well to people who come on too strong. Negotiating the wrong way could cost you the job."

— Bill Flavell, Senior VP,
International Business Development, RR Donnelly

18

Eight Things to do
if You Lose Your Job

The new reality: Three out of four executives lose a job at least once in their career. And, virtually everyone becomes reemployed. You can do it quickly and successfully while others will settle for much less than what they really deserve.

Today, unemployment is looked at from a far different perspective than in years past. For the most part, someone who becomes unemployed is viewed as a victim of economics beyond anyone's control.

Nevertheless, for those who lose their jobs, there can be a feeling of shock, disbelief, and even fear. It can mean the loss of many symbols of security that we take for granted. When we have a job, we have a place to go, an opportunity to achieve and people to work with, including close friends. Even in those cases where people resign, their initial feelings of self-confidence can quickly give way to concern and doubt if they don't land a new job quickly. Obviously, loss of income can also cause great apprehension.

Other people may not admit it, and may be quick to claim they quit all their previous positions, but many people who will interview you will have shared the same experience. Being fired, or asked to leave, doesn't mean failure in the eyes of everyone else, even though you may feel tremendously depressed. Don't let it give you a complex and, even more important, don't feel sorry for yourself.

At senior levels in business, there have been many terminated executives who have gone on to further success. For example, Bernard Marcus, founder and CEO of Home Depot, Jimmy Johnson, formerly of the Dallas Cowboys and now of the Miami Dolphins, and Rick Miller, formerly of Wang and recently CFO at AT&T.

The eight principles

If you lose a job, there are several steps that to take right away.

1. Start on your campaign immediately. Don't take a long vacation and don't retreat socially. Your advantage will be your ability to devote all of your time to job hunting. The best psychological boost you can get will come from having a schedule full of activity: breakfast meetings, lunches, interviews, letter writing, phone calls, and follow-ups. The way to do that is to get into action and give your job search top priority.

2. Get support from your employer. In addition to negotiating your outplacement assistance, the firm might even provide office space, secretarial help, and the use of a phone. You will also need to get total agreement on the reason for your separation. If there were negatives involved, work out an explanation that puts you in the best light. Look for clarification that the termination was due to factors beyond your control, such as a cutback, merger, or reorganization.

   By the way, never make the mistake of implying threats. If you are in a position to harm your employer, they will know about it without your saying so, and they'll be taking it into account in dealing with you.

3. Invest in your campaign right away. Ask for the type of outplacement assistance that will benefit you the most. If your firm refuses to provide help, you haven't lost anything. If they do, make sure you select the company, or ask to apply the funds they have allocated to the service of your choice.

4. Get access to an office phone. It helps to have a base of operations at an office. You might be able to use the number of a friend who can have his secretary take messages for you, or list a phone number under your own consulting service. At the very least, establish a work station in your home and let everyone know it is to be treated as your office.

5. Get yourself a friend who will be a source of encouragement and who can be a good sounding board. Share your progress and maintain communication with that person throughout the campaign.

6. Do a complete financial plan that assumes that you may be unemployed for quite a while. Allow sufficient funds to enable you to dress well, to get any professional help you need, and to actively pursue a job campaign.

7. Be as physically active as you can. Many people who have not been active have found that as more time passed, the less capable they were — psychologically and emotionally — to go out and do what must be done to win the right new job.

8. Don't be overanxious. Never beg for a position or try to explain your situation in print. Everyone likes to hire talent that is hard to find.

"No one is secure in today's job market. If you're earning above $100,000, there will come a time when your position is re-engineered or the company downsizes you out."

— The top HR Executive at one of
America's 20 largest companies

Handling liabilities

As important as your assets and skills are, you also need to be aware of anything that might be viewed as a shortcoming in the eyes of potential employers. Sometimes liabilities are overlooked. On other occasions they are mistakenly thought to be so serious that job hunters conclude that no corrective action can be taken.

To be successful, you should develop your strategy for handling any potential liability before you get involved in interviews. You know what your problem areas are. Give careful thought to how you should minimize their impact in all of your communications, both written and verbal.

By the way, some of the common liabilities that can cause a negative perception include: you're unemployed; you'll need to change industries; you've stayed too long with one employer; you're too old; you've changed jobs too often; you may be too generalized or too specialized; your career has peaked; your achievements aren't measurable; you lack experience in blue-chip firms; your jobs have been too similar; and your work history has gaps. Keep in mind that there is virtually no career problem that has not already been successfully resolved by someone else.

If you build your will to succeed, it will make the difference every time. Your positive attitude is what will drive you to do it sooner rather than later. It is the single most common thread among all winners. It will separate you from the tens of thousands who simply give up, settle for less or remain in unattractive situations.

"If you lose an executive job get a strong support structure. Remain flexible and use top flight materials. Reevaluate your campaign on a regular basis. Like a major league ball player, you're simply now a free agent."

— Senior VP, Major Health Care Firm

Now, it won't be news to you that if you truly believe in yourself, you will have the best possible chance of achieving the most you are capable of. So it's a good time to remind yourself of all the good things you have done, and what you can do in the future.

The best way to make things happen is simply to get into action. Too many people make excuses. If it's not a recession, then it's their industry. If not that, then their skills have been made obsolete by technology. If not that, there are too many people going after too few jobs. There is no end to the power of rationalizing. Of course, these people lose their will to succeed and become immobile.

If, on the other hand, you look at the lives of achievers in any field, you will see that in addition to positive expectations, another common thread is they are very active people. Taking action is in itself like taking an energy tonic. When people get into action, they no longer have time to worry about whether they will achieve their goal.

Don't let life go by without doing the things you really want. To get the right job, you need the right attitude to get going, as well as the determination to do your best. Then you need to project the right attitude with everyone you meet. In short, it's your attitude that makes the sale. It works!

"The beliefs we hold have a lot to do with the kind of world we experience. If you believe that firms are not hiring, you will pay attention to items about layoffs or declines in sales. If you believe there are many areas of opportunity, then you will seek out new companies, new products and the like."

— Stephanie Miller, Psychologist

EIGHT THINGS TO DO IF YOU EVER LOSE YOUR JOB

Outplacement/Marketing
Campaigns by Princeton/Masters

Our company is a consulting and marketing organization. Highly-skilled in the art of marketing professionals, we are distinctly different from other firms in our field, virtually all of which are counseling or psychology-oriented firms.

Unlike those firms, we utilize a marketing system we have pioneered, and which our consultants professionally facilitate. Combined with our National Center concept—this enables us to enjoy unique economies of scale, and to offer services that other firms cannot duplicate.

In essence, our method is one of aggressive and committed action—performed on people's behalf, rather than counseling them on how to write resumes, letters, do research, etc. Our approach also allows us a range of options which can be tailored to our clients needs.

Today, at our National Center just outside of Denver, Colorado, we maintain an extraordinary range and depth of professional staff... in a facility that represents the leading edge in our field. Each year, professionals and executives from throughout the United States, Europe, and the Pacific Rim are marketed through this major facility.

The investment required to develop our operation has exceeded ten million dollars... and our job-market research budget is more than $1,000,000. The concept we use is similar to other specialized organizations who attract a national clientele because of their expertise within a given industry... e.g., organizations as famous as the Pritikin Center and the Mayo Clinic, as well as prominent spas or firms which manage the careers of professional athletes.

We pride ourselves in our understanding of the career search challenges which six figure executives in today's market face. The service we offer has four phases—the first three of which are prepared in advance and presented to our clients in the course of a two-day visit with us at our National Center. The fourth phase is where we help market them until the land the right new position.

Step 1 of Our Service—We present a complete marketing plan on how each person should be marketed

Our staff analyzes each persons situation and develops a Marketing Plan for helping them find a new position. Our plans cover five key areas:

- **Assessment of marketability and income potential.** We start by surfacing every conceivable asset or work experience that can enhance a persons marketability and income potential. If any perceived liabilities exist, such as concerns over age, being too specialized or too generalized, or having income deficiencies... we develop corrective strategies for handling them.

- **Personalized job matching analysis and opportunity areas.** Our staff uncovers each persons full range of career and industry options, including a review of frontier industries, growth situations, and many other areas that they might not have identified for themself.

- **Advanced level action plans for getting interviews.** We develop a customized action plan for getting them the right interviews. This strategic "game plan" covers not only *what* needs to be done... but also *how*, *when*, and *where*. A complete step-by-step track, it makes our searches as fail-safe as experience can provide.

- **Customized interviewing strategy.** We prepare people for interviewing by helping to maximize their ability to quickly build personal chemistry, by giving them a communications strategy, and by doing video interview training when appropriate. Our goal here is to expand their self-esteem and confidence, making sure they are at their very best.

- **Our negotiating system and strategies.** The last part of our marketing plan involves helping make sure that people don't leave potential income on the negotiating table. We equip them with our proven "soft-sell" system for negotiating their best financial package.

Step 2 of Our Service—We professionally write the resumes and letters that each person's career search will require

In today's competitive market, a high percentage of executives need several resumes to generate maximum activity for themselves. For our clients, we typically prepare several custom biographies, materials which are highly distinctive and persuasive, and which qualify each client for the highest positions possible. Typically, we write all of the following, each with its own specific application.

■ **A mainstream biography.** This distinctive and highly-persuasive document has a range of applications with the marketing plans we design.

■ **An executive recruiter resume.** This special resume helps us get maximum activity for our clients with suggested recruiters that our research staff supplies.

■ **A spot-opportunity resume.** This is also a specialty resume, which is designed to produce maximum response in situations involving emerging opportunities.

■ **A CEO biography.** For many six-figure executives, this unique approach is very effective with high-level contacts, CEOs, board members etc.

■ **Other biographies.** In many cases we also develop materials to broaden people's background and to qualify them for opportunities outside of their specialties.

■ **Campaign marketing letters.** Here we draft everything from letters people might require for establishing a high level reference, to letters to CEOs... for motivating influential people, for contacting acquaintances, for setting up a reference for following up an interview... and so on. In most situations, 10–12 letters are prepared. Having these done in advance saves a great deal of time, making it much easier for people to move quickly when a situation presents itself. Besides hard copy, they are supplied on disk, thereby facilitating easy tailoring to meet each persons needs

Step 3 of Our Service—We develop research on leads, contacts, and executive openings

Our research capability can often save those we work for weeks and months of time. Here's just a sample.

- **Targeting high- probability employers.** We do this from information we have on over 10,000,000 firms, including many local and hard-to-find organizations.

- **Looking into growth firms**. We keep a special file of America's most exciting firms—identified via *Business Week, Forbes, Fortune, Barrons, Financial Week* etc.

- **Emerging high-tech firms**. We also keep a file covering little known, emerging high-tech firms.

- **Invaluable information on any major market.** Our newsmaker file reveals what's going on from a business viewpoint—in any major market.

- **The right recruiters to contact.** From 10,000 recruiters, we can pinpoint the ones for people to contact.

- **High-level executives to network.** From a special executive networking file, we can identify people who would be unusually high probabilities for helping out.

- **Openings on the Internet.** We can also help uncover extensive openings through a variety of lesser-known online sources, and on the Internet.

- **Information before your interviews.** Here we can supply financials on NYSE, AMSE, or NASDAQ firms, as well as key information on private firms.

- **24-hour research response.** Our research staff covers the job market every day. Our Client Services Center turns around requests from our clients *on 24 hour notice*.

- **Dramatically expanded market coverage.** We feel comfortable that, with our resources, clients can access up to 90% of their true market... as opposed to current research stating that most individuals only achieve 10% to 15% market penetration.

Step 4 of Our Service—We manage the implementation of each campaign, and provide support every step of the way

At Princeton/Masters, we help clients from all over the world. Here's what we do, on an ongoing basis, to support them through their search:

■ **Weekly mailings to support them.** We prepare weekly laser-quality mailings to employers, recruiters, or ads people wish to answer. Here, we assist with a selective distribution of their credentials, designed to get their ability to contribute in front of the right people.

■ **Office space and administrative support.** We arrange for this type of support as needed.

■ **Printing.** We arrange for the quality printing of professional, personalized stationery to match each persons resume, and can print their resume as well.

■ **Reference checking.** If people have even the slightest concern, we can validate their references.

■ **Consulting help every step of the way.** Our staff team can be in a persons corner and available to strategize each situation that presents itself, as well as assisting throughout all negotiations.

In summary, our commitment is to work closely with everyone we assist until they accept the right new job.

The Princeton/Masters
Ten-Year Career Management Program

Once a person is a client of Princeton/Masters, they are eligible for assistance under our Ten-Year Career Management Program... a valuable service option which entitles them to privileges throughout their career. As part of this program, five levels of assistance are available.

■ **Complete redo of our service at no cost.** If a person wishes to change jobs again within the first year of our engagement, we will provide all professional elements of our service again.

■ **Annual career reassessments.** For up to ten years, they may contact us for a complete annual reassessment of their situation. Furthermore, if a career change is contemplated at any time, they may call us for our advice.

■ **Resume updates.** When we do their reassessments, we will update their main resume upon request.

■ **Access to job market research.** To assist in a future job search, they may also simultaneously access a full research selection from our national employer, recruiter and other databases as may be available.

■ **Free copies of our annually-updated publications.**

Our Ten-Year Career Management Program clearly underscores the degree of client commitment we make to each person we assist, and the ongoing relationship the firm enjoys with men and women from all fields who become our clients.

For more information

In our world of overnight deliveries, faxes, and advanced telecommunications, we can help organizations and individuals throughout the world, and regardless of anindividual's industry, career field, or location. For descriptive literature or more information, call Gordon Edwards at 800-770-1170, or fax your resume to him at 303-721-6617.